Yesterday's Chicago

Herman Kogan

Rick Kogan

Seemann's Historic Cities Series

No. 1: *Yesterday's Tampa* by Hampton Dunn

No. 2: *Yesterday's Miami* by Nixon Smiley

No. 3: *Yesterday's St. Petersburg* by Hampton Dunn

No. 4: *Yesterday's Key West* by Stan Windhorn & Wright Langley

No. 5: *Yesterday's Sarasota* by Del Marth

No. 6: *Yesterday's Clearwater* by Hampton Dunn

No. 7: *Yesterday's Tallahassee* by Hampton Dunn

No. 8: *Yesterday's Atlanta* by Franklin M. Garrett

No. 9: *Yesterday's Detroit* by Frank Angelo

No. 10: *Yesterday's Denver* by Sandra Dallas

No. 11: *Yesterday's Cape Cod* by Evelyn Lawson

No. 12: *Yesterday's Florida Keys* by Stan Windhorn & Wright Langley

No. 13: *Yesterday's Philadelphia* by George Wilson

No. 14: *Yesterday's Akron* by Kenneth Nichols

No. 15: *Yesterday's Fort Myers* by Marion Godown & Alberta Rawchuck

No. 16: *Yesterday's Nashville* by Carl Zibart

No. 17: *Yesterday's Asheville* by Joan & Wright Langley

No. 18: *Yesterday's Birmingham* by Malcolm C. McMillan

No. 19: *Yesterday's Cincinnati* by Luke Feck

No. 20: *Yesterday's Bradenton* by Arthur C. Schofield

No. 21: *Yesterday's San Diego* by Neil Morgan & Tom Blair

No. 22: *Yesterday's Chicago* by Herman & Rick Kogan

No. 23: *Yesterday's Milwaukee* by Robert W. Wells

No. 24: *Yesterday's Washington, D. C.* by Charles Ewing

No. 25: *Yesterday's Memphis* by Charles W. Crawford

No. 26: *Yesterday's Los Angeles* by Norman Dash

No. 27: *Yesterday's Augusta* by Ray Rowland & Helen Callahan

No. 28: *Yesterday's Lexington* by Eric Karnes

No. 29: *Yesterday's Palm Beach* by Stuart McIver

No. 30: *Yesterday's Cleveland* by George E. Condon

HERMAN KOGAN & RICK KOGAN

Yesterday's

CHICAGO

Seemann's Historic Cities Series No. 22

E. A. Seemann Publishing, Inc.
Miami, Florida

THE ILLUSTRATIONS in this book came from many sources, all indicated in abbreviated form at the end of each caption. They included public and private collections, city agencies, commercial firms, educational and cultural institutions, volumes long out of print, newspaper libraries, archives, and various individuals. Below, with our gratitude, is a guide to these sources.

AI	Art Institute of Chicago	GP	George Peebles
AP	Associated Press	HFM	Henry Ford Museum
CAC	Chicago Association of Commerce and Industry	IBT	Illinois Bell Telephone Company
		IC	Illinois Central Railroad
CAM	*Chicago and its Makers*	IH	International Harvester
CBA	Chicago Bar Association	JA	Jane Addams Allen
CDN	*Chicago Daily News*	JAMC	Jane Addams Memorial Collection
CDUR	Chicago Department of Urban Renewal	KC	Kogan Collection
CFD	Chicago Fire Department	MBI	Moody Bible Institute
CHS	Chicago Historical Society	MF	Dr. Morris Fishbein
CPC	Chicago Plan Commission	MNP	Metro News Photos
CPD	Chicago Police Department	MSI	Museum of Science and Industry
CPL	Chicago Public Library	PGC	Peoples Gas Company
CPPA	Chicago Press Photographers Assoc.	PR	Pennsylvania Railroad
CST	*Chicago Sun-Times*	RF	Ralph Frost
CTA	Chicago Transit Authority	SDS	Shirlee De Santi
DT	Danny Thomas	SR	Sears Roebuck and Company
EM	Edward McGill	UA	United Airlines
FEA	Field Enterprises Archives	UC	University of Chicago
FNB	First National Bank of Chicago	WKC	Wendt-Kogan Collection
FT	Fred Townsend	WS	William Sturm Collection

Library of Congress Cataloging in Publication Data

Kogan, Herman.
    Yesterday's Chicago.

    (Seemann's historic cities series ; no. 22)
    Includes index.
    1. Chicago—History—Pictorial works.
2. Chicago—Description—Views. I. Kogan, Rick,
joint author. II. Title.
F548.37.K63   977.3'11'00222   76-10381
ISBN 0-912458-65-8

For M'Loo
Whom we love

Contents

Foreword | 9
Someday, A Great City: Origins to 1872 | 11
From Calamity to Celebration: 1872 to 1893 | 35
Triumphs and Tumults: 1893 to 1920 | 67
The Years That Roared: 1920 to 1933 | 115
Problems and Progress: 1933 to 1955 | 149
Index | 199

Foreword

OUR AIM in these pages is not only to trace the history of our favorite city but to convey its flavor and tone at specific periods in its turbulent lifetime until the mid-1950s. Consequently, in addition to people, places, and events that formed that history, we present many others perhaps not historically crucial who have contributed to Chicago's reputation, for good or ill, giving it a renown that has made it more often studied, praised, criticized, denounced, and admired than other American cities.

If, even within these space limits, we are able to add to one's knowledge through pictures and words about vital elements in the city's saga, we will have fulfilled part of our function. If we evoke nostalgic memories and recollections, we will be gratified. Our hope is that Chicago's past comes alive again for all who course through this volume.

A full listing of individuals and institutions helpful in gathering illustrations and information appears elsewhere, but we must single out those who went beyond the call of duty and friendship.

Early in our research we asked members of the Chicago Press Photographers Association (CPPA) for their cooperation, and foremost in response were such skilled veterans as Ralph Frost, Edward McGill, and George Peebles, many of whose striking works are included. Also there are photographs of another CPPA stalwart, the late William Sturm, and we are grateful to his widow, Mrs. Armin Hennigs, for making them available. Robert Kotalik, chief photographer for the *Sun-Times* and a longtime CPPA officer, assisted in tracking down photographs of the 1920-1950 years.

Newspaper colleagues gave varied aid: Emmett Dedmon, vice-president and editorial director of the newspaper division of Field Enterprises, Inc. (publisher of the *Sun-Times* and *Daily News*), made available his impressively detailed notes for his popular history, *Fabulous Chicago*. Ben Kopriva of the *Sun-Times* art department was a wise and patient counselor, as were the paper's photo editor, Maurie Falstein, and its librarian, Janice Lewis, and her staff. Bob Herguth and Harlan Draeger of the *Daily News* helped considerably. As ever, Shirlee De Santi of the *Sun-Times* was invaluable to the project's completion. Don Wehner of the *New Buffalo Times* in Michigan furnished technical assistance, and Lloyd Wendt, *Tribune* editorial executive and fellow-author, offered sound advice in several areas.

City officials whose cooperation was essential and whose contributions were appreciated included Police Supt. James M. Rochford and his department's public relations director, Tina Vicini; Alice Gorman of the Department of Urban Renewal; Patrick Cunningham of the Department of Development and Planning; and Thomas Buck and Robert D. Heinlein of the Chicago Transit Authority.

Most productive among those associated with Chicago companies were Joseph O'Brien, J. B. Sutter, and Ellen Guske of the Illinois Bell Telephone Company; J. P. Daneluk of International Harvester; Patricia M. Wees of Peoples Gas Company; and Lenore Swoiskin of Sears, Roebuck and Company. Wally Phillips of WGN made on-the-air comments about the project that resulted in several valuable leads to material. For a previous project, Eugene I. Stein, Jr., had permitted access to the copious files of Kaufmann and Fabry, and that boon yielded important materials for this one. Marilyn McCree of the Jane Addams Memorial Collection and Jane Addams Allen furnished rare photographs from their respective files.

We are extremely grateful for assistance of various kinds given by Mark Kogan, whose affiliation with us had to be curtailed by the press of other duties, and by Marilew Kogan, who shared our hopes, enthusiasm, problems, and toil.

Herman and Rick Kogan

Chicago
October 1976

THIS RARE MAP of 1812 spots Fort Dearborn and other points of interest in the sparsely settled area, such as the cabins of French-Canadian trader Antoine Ouilmette and of Thomas Burns, a soldier who had served out his enlistment at the fort, and the dwelling area of the Potawatomis, whose friendliness had turned to hostility from what they considered harsh treatment and betrayals by their white neighbors. (KC)

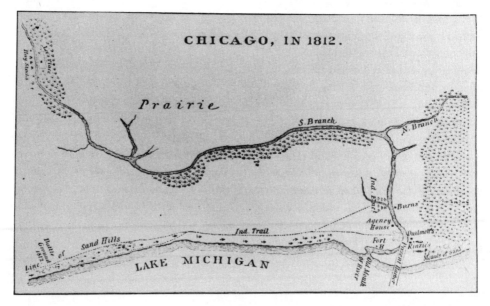

Someday, a Great City: Origins to 1872

IN THE HISTORY of the birth of Midwestern cities in the eighteenth and early nineteenth centuries and the gradual urbanization of America, Chicago has had a remarkable career. Over the decades it has far outstripped others whose early promise seemed as bright or brighter. This was due to certain natural advantages—a vitally strategic location, for one thing—but other compelling factors influenced its destiny: a fiercely competitive spirit, a hunger for riches, a strong sense of pride, a drive for power, an audacity, an excess of vigor, an ability to rebound from adversity.

Youngest of the world's great cities, it was not officially incorporated until 1837. But, long before that time, events and people had attested to its special qualities and contributed to its lore, legends, and realities.

Millions of years ago, when the last great ice field retreated and left behind a lake that gradually subsided into a larger one, Lake Michigan, there was ultimately created a stretch of sodden ground that would come to be called the Chicago Portage, nine miles long and connecting a winding creek and the Des Plaines River, a waterway to the Illinois and eventually to the mighty Mississippi. Indians lived here for many generations, hunting game on the prairies and warring with each other for possession of this crossing place. The Algonquins, fleeing the ferocious Iroquois, came to the eastern end of the portage and, looking about them, smelled the skunk cabbage and wild onion on the banks of the river that flowed into Lake Michigan. Imbedded legend has it—and only the crankiest purist will quibble—that they thereupon affixed to the site the Indian word for those earth products: *Checagou* or, as some versed deeply in Indian speech maintain, *Eschikagou.*

The first white men known to have come to the portage and the site of the future city were French. One was Fr. Jacques Marquette, who had established the Jesuit mission of St. Ignace at the Straits of Mackinac in 1671 although his six predecessors sent to Christianize the tribes had felt the horrors of Iroquois torture stakes. In the winter of 1672, he was joined there by Louis Joliet (also Jolliet), a Canadian-born explorer commis-

ROBERT THOM

THE CROSSING PLACE: The first white men to use the Chicago Portage were Fr. Jacques Marquette and Louis Joliet in 1673. On their way back from a vain effort to find a water route in the New World for their monarch Louis XIV, they came upon a village of friendly Illinois Indians, as depicted by Robert Thom, and the tribesmen escorted them across the portage linking the Chicago and DesPlaines rivers. (IBT)

sioned to explore the Mississippi River in the name of Louis XIV in the hope that it would be a southerly route to the Orient. They set out with five other men, eventually learning that the hope was a vain one and heading back for fear of encountering enemies if they went as far as the Gulf of Mexico.

While their companions continued back to the mission, Father Marquette and Joliet paddled alone up the Illinois River. At Ottawa they found a large Indian village, to whose inhabitants Father Marquette preached. Then guides led them to the Des Plaines River and onto the Chicago Portage and to where the Chicago River met Lake Michigan. Joliet wrote an enthusiastic report, urging that a canal be dug across the portage for, as he predicted, "Here will some day be found one of the world's great cities."

Although Father Marquette returned the next winter and various other explorers and traders used the portage route frequently on journeys westward, the French did nothing to capitalize on the explorers' evaluations. Another French missionary, Fr. François Pinet, did establish, in 1696, the Mission of the Guardian Angel, working diligently for four years with the Miamis, a tribe that had settled in two nearby villages to escape the Iroquois. And a later adventurer shared his predecessors' vision: "This will be the gate of empire," declaimed Robert Cavalier, sieur de la Salle, standing at the tip of the portage. "This will be the seat of commerce. The typical man who will grow up here must be an enterprising man. Each day, as he rises, he will exclaim, 'I act, I move, I push!'"

[12]

For much of the eighteenth century Chicago was literally in a void. Indian tribes fought each other, and the French, at war with the English, gave even less attention to their lands in America. Chicago lay beyond civilization, undisturbed by British ships plying the Great Lakes. A peace treaty in 1763 ceded the entire region to the English, but they ignored proposals to build a fort at Chicago and plan for the future.

While Chicago was part of George III's empire, the man now acknowledged to be its authentic founder made his entrance. He was Jean Baptiste Pointe du Sable, a French-speaking black man from Santo Domingo, Haiti, who began trading with the Indians in 1772 and by 1779 was firmly established on the north bank of the river mouth at Lake Michigan. A man of culture, taste, and refinement, du Sable married a Potawatomi woman—sometimes he jested that he was actually a Potawatomi chief—and filled his handsome log house with fine furniture and art works, cleared a white oak forest for a cornfield, and worked the land in addition to trading for furs with the Indians.

Du Sable was prospering when, in the summer of 1795, Indian tribes defeated in battle by troops led by Gen. Anthony Wayne ("Mad Anthony" of Revolutionary War fame) gathered at Fort Grenville in western Ohio to sign a peace treaty. By its terms, various tracts of land were ceded to the relatively new United States on which to build forts—one at Peoria, another at the mouth of the Illinois River, and a third at Chicago. What historian Milo M. Quaife would much later call "the most momentous real estate transaction in the history of Chicago" was simply stated: "One piece of land Six Miles square at the mouth of the Chicago River emptying into the southwest end of Lake Michigan."

A year later du Sable was joined in his enterprises by a French-Canadian, Antoine Ouilmette, a trapper and boatman also married to a Potawatomi woman. And four years later, du Sable, quite wealthy now, suddenly sold his house and post to Jean Le Lime (also La Lime) and moved to Missouri, where he lived the life of a substantial citizen until his death in 1814.

In the early spring of 1803, the first men wearing the uniforms of the United States arrived in Chicago under command of Capt. John Whistler. Their mission was to build a

FOR MANY YEARS the role in Chicago history of Jean Baptiste Pointe du Sable *(below right)*, a black man from Haiti, was obscure, although in the 1770s he had established the first permanent residence, and flourished as a trader with the Indians until he departed in 1800. Long labeled the founder of Chicago, John Kinzie *(below left),* a hard-eyed entrepreneur from Canada, arrived in 1804, bought du Sable's house from an intermediary, and became prominent in the region until his death in 1828. In the light of later discoveries, the credit has been given to du Sable. (FEA-CHS)

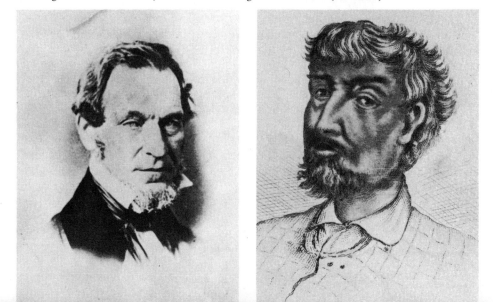

fort that would not only be the local garrison but would guard the portage. Its name: Fort Dearborn, after U.S. Secretary of War Henry Dearborn. Sweating through that summer and fall, Whistler and his men raised the fort on the south bank of the Chicago River. With it finished, more settlers started arriving, and most prominent among them was John Kinzie, a canny fur trader originally from Quebec who bought the du Sable house from Le Lime shortly after arriving early in 1804. Soon he and his wife Eleanor were the leading civilian family in the settlement, and Kinzie was also active at Fort Dearborn as a kind of banker-provisioner (50 cents for a quart of liquor or a pound of butter or tobacco). Kinzie, a rapacious sort, maintained an on-again, off-again partnership with Captain Whistler and, after Whistler was recalled to Detroit, Kinzie had a rancorous relationship with the new commander, Capt. Nathan Heald. Bad blood between Kinzie and Le Lime, now an interpreter at the fort, led to a knife fight that proved fatal to Le Lime; Kinzie pleaded self-defense and was acquitted.

The first great tragedy in Chicago's history soon occurred. In the War of 1812, sixty-year-old William Hull was put in charge of American forces in the Midwest. The English won the Indians to their side and, early in August, General Hull, having heard of the surrender of Fort Mackinac and fearing depredations, sent orders out to evacuate all frontier outposts, including Fort Dearborn. Many of the garrison force wanted to stay behind and give supplies to the Indians, which would entail a financial loss for Kinzie. When Capt. William Wells, an experienced scout, arrived to supervise the fort's evacuation, he found much confusion. Captain Heald had already distributed some goods to the Potawatomis as a guarantee of safe conduct, but when the whiskey and guns that belonged to Kinzie were dumped into the river at Kinzie's behest, Black Partridge, a friendly Potawatomi, warned Captain Heald that he would not be able to restrain the more impetuous of his braves.

Nevertheless, on the morning of August 15, a straggling group of some one hundred comprising militiamen, soldiers, Kinzie and other settlers and their wives and children, plus a band of Miamis, left the fort and moved slowly southward along the beach. They had gone barely two miles when warriors daubed with paint fell upon them, and in the brief-but-bloody massacre all 12 militiamen, 26 of the 55 regulars, 2 women, and all the children were slain. Though badly wounded, Wells fought on until a brave named Peesotum killed him, scalped him, and divided his heart with another, both eating it in the belief they would acquire Wells' courage. Kinzie, his wife, his stepdaughter Mrs. Margaret Helms, and Mrs. Heald managed to escape to St. Joseph, with the aid of Indians who had a boat waiting for them by the river. On the next night, Fort Dearborn was set afire while warriors stomped and shrieked and by morning all that remained intact was the fort's powder magazine.

The Kinzies were back again in 1816 when a new Fort Dearborn was built, larger and more fortified than its predecessor. New settlers trickled into the territory and, although the general atmosphere was languid, there were those who echoed the earlier promising opinions. In 1820, Henry Schoolcraft, a government mineralogist touring the area with Lewis Cass, governor-general of the Michigan Territory, wrote, "The country around

FORT DEARBORN is being built in the fall of 1803 under the direction of Capt John Whistler and his engineer, Lt. James Strode Swearingen. George Parish, Jr.'s rendition is of a scene when completion seemed an easy prospect, but lack of building equipment caused delays, and food supplies were skimpy. John Kinzie, adept at trading with the Indians, came to Whistler's aid by securing him food and other essentials. When it was finally finished toward the end of 1804, the fort, in the words of one British visitor, was "the neatest and best garrison in the country." Nearby, as shown in the engraving below from A. T. Andreas' classic history of Chicago, was Kinzie's enlarged house. (IBT-KC)

REBEKAH HEALD was the young wife of Capt. Nathan Heald, commander of Fort Dearborn in the War of 1812. Despite warnings by friendly Potawatomis that the more hostile braves among them would attack, Heald evacuated the fort on the fateful morning of August 15, 1812, as ordered by his superiors who feared it might fall into British hands. In the subsequent savage assault, many were killed, but Mrs. Heald, pictured here in an ultra-dramatic version, proved quite a fighter. She was wounded and carried away by a friendly chief named Cheecheebingway, also known as Alexander Robinson, and then spirited off with the Kinzie family by other friendly Indians. Captain Heald and others were taken by the British, but later released, and he and his wife were reunited. (CPL)

Chicago is the most fertile and beautiful that can be imagined. . . . To the ordinary advantages of an agricultural marketing town it must hereafter add that of a depot for inland commerce between the northern and southern sections of the Union, and a great thoroughfare for strangers, merchants and travelers." These sentiments were expressed two years after Illinois had achieved statehood, and there were, true enough, many strangers, merchants, and travelers who did not agree and who, after a look at the rather somnolent little community centering around a fort, went on to Galena, Kaskaskia, or Vandalia in the new state, or beyond to St. Louis or Cincinnati, well-established cities that they were certain would always be superior. Such doubters would be proved wrong.

The 1820s were relatively uneventful, except that Congress did fund the building of the canal that Joliet had envisioned—a project that would be some twenty years in the making, and with less than happy results. Then, in 1832 came a new conflict with the Indians, this time with the forces of Black Hawk, a mighty Sauk chief determined to regain ceded hunting grounds in Illinois and surrounding regions. Fort Dearborn, defended only by armed militiamen, was packed with frightened families. Cholera struck in and around the town. Yet the war, ending quickly that August when the Illinois militia virtually destroyed Black Hawk's warriors, had a salutary effect. Gen. Winfield Scott, commanding troops sent against Black Hawk, recommended to the War Department that a harbor be built at Chicago, and a young Southern army engineer, Jefferson Davis, backed it up with technical data that persuaded Congress to appropriate $24,000 to dredge the Chicago River and create an anchorage for shipping. By treaty, the region was cleared of hostile Potawatomi, Ottawa, and Chippewa tribes. Chicago was now the seat of newly created Cook County. And the boom of the 1830s was on the way.

THE BEAUBIEN BROTHERS were early settlers in the tiny community that centered around new Fort Dearborn, built in 1816. Following his brother Jean, a clever agent for John Jacob Astor's American Fur Company, jolly and affable Mark *(right)* came down from Detroit in the early 1820s and was soon the area's prime host. (CPL)

Soldiers who had chased Indians across the adjoining prairies or paused on their way to battle went back home to report well of the verdant land. Newcomers arrived, knapsacks on their backs or burlap bags in hand, by stagecoach and by wagon. From the East the way was via the Erie Canal or through the Mohawk pass to Buffalo, thence by schooners and steamboats on the Great Lakes to the new Chicago harbor. Land values in 1833 soared wildly; a parcel of land on Lake Street, developing into a street of merchants, that was worth $300 at the start of the year went for $60,000 by the end of the year. Young John Stephen Wright came from Galena, joined a friend in buying two acres of swamp for $50, and continued to acquire more land until by 1834, at only nineteen, he was worth $200,000 and became an undying Chicago Booster. On August 5, 1833, the 200 taxpayers met and incorporated Chicago as a village and on the following November 26, the

MARK BEAUBIEN took over the grubby Eagle Exchange, a tavern at Lake and Market streets, made repairs, added rooms, and renamed it The Sauganash Inn in honor of Billy Caldwell, an Indian chief whose tribal name was Sauganash. Foremost in the area, this hotel was where trustees met in 1833 to incorporate Chicago as a village, and here, too, gayety prevailed, for Mark was a fine fiddler and a lusty balladeer. Though some complained that his liquor was inferior, that he was stingy with his blankets, and that his rooms were infested with rats, Beaubien was able to lure guests from rival establishments. (CPL)

[17]

first issue of the *Democrat,* the city's first newspaper, advised that over one hundred and fifty buildings had gone up since the start of the year and that 20,000 had swept through this Chicago that was described by a visitor as "a chaos of mud, rubbish and confusion."

Soon enough, in 1835, there was another newspaper, the *American,* announcing that 2,000 transients were in the village seeking employment. William B. Ogden, a buoyant young member of the New York state legislature, came to look at some land a relative had bought, caught the fever and stayed on after selling the property at a substantial profit. A doughty lawyer named Stephen A. Douglas left his law practice in downstate Jacksonville and bought 100 acres of sand-dunes land south of the village. New stores and new houses went up along main streets—La Salle, Dearborn, Clark, and Lake. John Kinzie's son John, Jr., his nephew, and Gurdon S. Hubbard, who had reaped riches in real estate since arriving in 1819 at sixteen, and others of the newly wealthy built mansions along Michigan Avenue facing the lake. In 1836, when work actually started on the Illinois and Michigan Canal, speculation soared and parcels of land alongside or near the proposed channel brought crazy prices. Chicago was not yet a city but it surely was a real estate capital. Joseph N. Balestier, a young lawyer, reported that he was earning $500 a day making out land titles. "The physicians threw physic to the dogs," he wrote to a friend, "and wrote promissory notes instead of prescriptions. Even the day laborer has become learned in the mysteries of quit-claim and warranty." And Harriet Martineau,

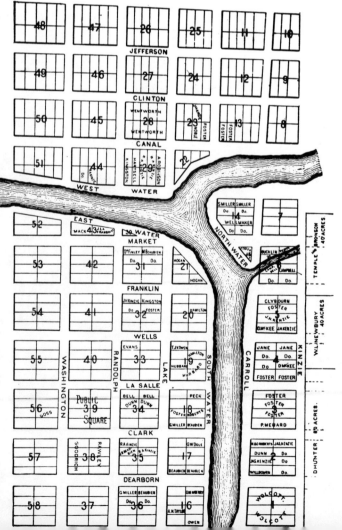

WHEN THE FEDERAL GOVERNMENT authorized construction of the Illinois and Michigan Canal, destined to cut across the Chicago Portage, James Thompson, an army surveyor, was assigned to plat the settlement, which contained less than one hundred residents. Although it would be a long time before work on the canals would start, his sketch of August 1830 had historical significance since he called the settlement the "Town of Chicago," the first time that name was officially used. (IC)

THE FIRST COURTHOUSE, essential to the rush of business emanating from the land boom of the early 1830s and other legal matters, was put up in 1835. It had a courtroom seating 200 on the first floor and a basement with offices and cells. The brick structure stood at Clark and Randolph streets, and those pigs seen here often clambered up its steps and blocked the doorway. (KC)

arriving from England that winter, was astonished at what she saw: "The streets are crowded with land speculators. . . . As the gentlemen of our party walked the streets, storekeepers hailed them with offers of farms and all manner of corner lots."

As if in celebration, Chicago officially became a city on March 4, 1837, in the Saloon Building. And then the bubble burst. No sooner had Ogden been elected Chicago's first mayor shortly thereafter than financial panic, already sweeping through the East, hit the new city. Illinois went bankrupt. Work on the canal stopped. But Ogden, even while noting the financial wreckage of some of the quick fortunes, refused to be daunted. "Bankruptcy is a disgrace!" he cried, and he borrowed money from sound banks on his personal credit and used it to pay the city's bills. He urged citizens caught in the debacle to grow their own gardens, and soon the city had its steadfast motto, *Urbs in Horto* – City in a Garden. Business houses issued their own scrip in the emergency. Local insurance firms issued certificates of deposit that were used as money. The city teetered, but did not succumb, although land values dropped from $10 million to $1 million within months and many investors were wiped out.

And still the population grew. From the 100 clustered near Fort Dearborn in 1830, the figure grew to 4,470 in 1840, the year the city's free school system was established. It was a gratifying growth but not without inevitable problems. For along with the Boomers and the Boosters came the hoodlums, rowdies, thieves, pickpockets, burglars, gamblers, and prostitutes. Not until two years after Ogden's election was there a single paid constable or policemen. There were a great many saloons: "I have never seen a town which seems so like a universal grog shop," lamented John Hankins, a temperance movement leader. On the north side of the river, not far from the lake, lay the Sands, a gathering of brothels, vice dens, and gambling holes.

AN EARLY STRUCTURE of importance, the Saloon Building at Lake and Clark streets was so named because its upper floor held a hall, or salon, that was the largest west of Buffalo. In 1837, Chicago received its city charter in it and, until 1843, another room served as City Hall, with councilmen meeting there regularly to debate a growing array of problems. Later, the building served variously as the local post office, the area's first United States District Court (until 1857), and as an auditorium where orators and debaters thundered, and concerts, dramatic performances, and other entertainments were staged. (CAM)

[20]

CHICAGO'S FIRST MAYOR: A native New Yorker, William B. Ogden arrived during the boom times of the early 1830s and became rich in land deals. He was affiliated with virtually all the fledgling city's first developments, notably the construction of the Galena & Chicago Union Railroad that in 1848 set Chicago on the road to greatness as the nation's premier rail center. (CHS)

OGDEN'S RAILROAD initially ran less than ten miles, never reaching Galena with its first locomotive, the "Pioneer." Within weeks after that run on October 10, 1848, Ogden and his associates put up their station, Chicago's first, along the north branch of the Chicago River, and gradually the line extended westward, including feeder lines that tapped the Northwest's grain fields. The infant railroad even had a slogan, "The Best of Everything," and it endured through years of change and growth after becoming the Chicago and North Western Railway. (KC)

A MORE EXTENSIVE LINE was the Illinois Central, first to link Chicago with the South. In 1850, Stephen A. Douglas, representing Illinois in the U.S. Senate, led a successful campaign for Congress to grant the state more than two and a half million acres to build a railroad. A group of Eastern capitalists, with some support from wealthy local men, organized the Illinois Central Railroad Company, with the proviso that seven per cent of yearly gross receipts go to the state. Work began in 1851, with rails brought from England through New Orleans, the Erie Canal, and the Great Lakes. Over 100,000 laborers came from the East to lay down the first 366 miles of track between Chicago and downtown Cairo and, by 1856, the Illinois Central was the longest road in the country. This print shows the IC tracks along the city's lake shore in 1860. (IC)

CYRUS HALL McCORMICK *(left),* a native Virginian who in 1831 perfected a mechanical reaper, spent years fighting the claims of rival inventors, making improvements, and licensing manufactures in various towns. In 1847, to concentrate production, he built a single plant at a cost of $600,000 on the north bank of the Chicago River not far from Lake Michigan. It was a wise decision, for it started the McCormick dynasty. He promoted vigorously, sent out salesmen to the farmlands, and often appeared himself to demonstrate his products, most impressively in 1851 at the Crystal Palace exhibition in London. By 1856 his plant *(above)* was turning out over five thousand reapers a year, all guaranteed with a then-unique, money-back offer if not found satisfactory. (IH)

But recovery was in prospect. Products from the new farms came in a steady stream. By 1838 Chicago shipped its first thirty-eight bags of wheat to the East, and a year later, as the panic was drawing to an end, the new firm of Newberry and Dole shipped 1,678 bushels of wheat in its brig *Osceola.* John Stephen Wright, with characteristic buoyancy, disclosed that although he had lost $100,000, he was not saddened: "I came here with nothing. I could have lost a million."

By 1843 the city was again on its feet. Grain elevators multiplied along the river banks. Wheat shipments swelled enormously, and the city was on its way to becoming the world's largest grain market. The hogs and cattle coming across the prairies went to crude slaughterhouses, forerunners of the Union Stock Yards of twenty years hence, to be converted into pork and beef for metropolises, even London. The Illinois and Michigan Canal, finally finished in 1848, was not the wonder of wonders it had aimed to be, but it was more than adequate for farmers and stockmen, formerly compelled to cross muddy stretches, to have their wares hauled by barges or other shallow-draft vessels. When a New Orleans newspaper, *De Bow's Weekly,* learned that cargoes by way of the canal reached Buffalo two weeks before those on the New Orleans-New York-Erie Canal route, it called

Chicago "an enemy," but had praise for its "energy, enterprise, and indomitable spirit" and its "system of bold, vigorous and sustained efforts." Even more important in this decade, though, was the beginning of Chicago as a railroad center, an ambition nurtured by Ogden from his earliest days in the city. Only six months after the opening of the canal, Ogden's dinky little Galena & Chicago Union Railroad train made its maiden run of ten miles, and the *Democrat* recorded: "A number of gentlemen rode upon the cars and all parties appeared satisfied with the road so far."

That satisfaction would last a long time. Within two years the tracks were extended, and two years later again. And by then, in 1852, the Illinois Central and the Rock Island roads were under construction. By mid-decade, ten trunk lines stretched in and out of the city, and eleven branch lines. In the short span of seven years, with nearly one hundred trains coming and going each day, Chicago had leaped into command as the nation's rail center, a distinction it was never to lose.

The railroads transformed the city more crucially and vividly—and lastingly—than any other development. They made of it a huge wholesale market from which hundreds of cities and towns could draw their wants of every kind. They stimulated the rise of new businesses, larger department stores, factories, plants, and other enterprises of enduring significance. And they brought more inhabitants. In a single year, 1853, the population jumped from 38,734 to 60,662, many of the newcomers immigrants from Europe. By the decade's end, there were 109,260 people crowded inside the city limits, four times as many as ten years earlier.

CHICAGO IN 1853: In two decades what had started as a swamp town was now a teeming city that liked to think of itself as "Queen of the Lakes." Newcomers arrived hourly. At the time of this very imaginative drawing the population was 60,662, twice as much as in 1850, and the whole decade was a period of intense growth. Its defects were innumerable, but its boosters were vociferous. In 1853 there were thirty newspapers, most constantly singing the city's praises while editorially calling for onslaughts against crime. (KC)

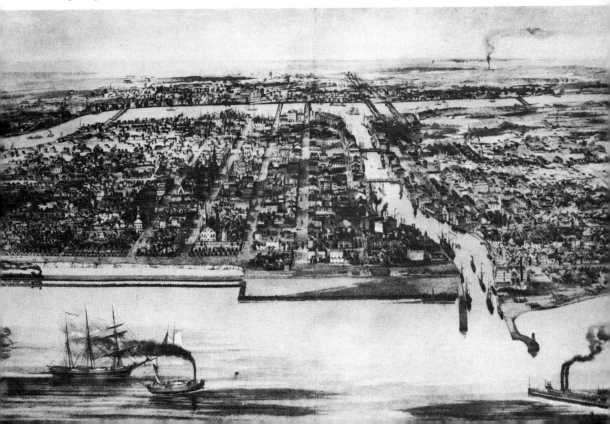

IN 1856, three years after Alexander Hesler came to Chicago from Galena, he was hard at work photographing everything in sight, including reconstructed Fort Dearborn, just before it was demolished the next year. Across the river can be seen Lake House, then a much-patronized riverside inn. (CHS)

LATER, HESLER LUGGED his camera to the courthouse tower, then the city's highest point, and aimed in all directions to create a remarkable panoramic series. Here, Randolph Street is in the foreground with the Sherman House, a most popular hostelry, bordered on the left by a row of taverns and eating places. Above, to the north, mercantile houses are visible on Lake Street a block away, and far beyond is the fast-growing residential district of the near North Side. The cupola atop the Sherman House served as more than an ornament; men sat in it, as in similar ones on other hotels, to detect incoming boats and trains by telescope, so that omnibuses could be speedily sent to pick up potential guests. (CHS)

A FAR LESS SAVORY sector of the turbulent city in the 1850s was the Sands, a stretch of lakeshore near the river on which were some twenty cheap lodging houses, brothels, and gambling dens. Despite outcries, nothing was done about them until John "Long John" Wentworth was elected mayor in March 1857. After warnings to such rulers of the grisly domain as Dutch Frank and John and Mary Hill, said to be originators of the badger game, he led in a band of policemen and vigilantes, ordered occupants of the various places to leave, and then demolished the shanties and ramshackle dwellings. Fires also broke out in other buildings and, by evening, most of what the *Tribune* called "this congregation of the vilest haunts of the most depraved and degraded creatures in our city" had been wiped out. (CHS-KC)

POTTER PALMER *(left)*, twenty-six when he arrived in 1852 and eager to become an important storekeeper, opened a dry-goods shop on Lake Street, where he permitted returns of merchandise found unacceptable, advertised heavily, and fashioned attractive displays, all innovations for the time. When he took in two young partners, Marshall Field *(below right)*, and Levi Z. Leiter *(below left)*, they followed his lead, improved on it, and after Palmer's retirement from the business, became the city's prime merchants. Palmer's later ventures were in real estate. He transformed State Street from a creaky road into the main thoroughfare by buying up property and building the first Palmer House and thirty-two other buildings. (KC-FEA)

Even with civic planning, of which there was very little, the pressures would have been heavy. Cries for better police protection, better water, improved fire-fighting methods, and cleaner politics resounded throughout the decade. Crime was rampant: "The city is at the mercy of its criminal classes," shrilled the *Tribune.* Nevertheless, when John Wentworth, the famous "Long John," with bluster and bravado became mayor in 1857 and tried to clean up the town, he found the problem insurmountable. So, while material progress was being made, Chicago was also getting a reputation as one of the wickedest cities in the land.

Financial panic once more struck in 1857, with inevitable business failures, runs on banks, and a rise in unemployment. But the calamity did not hinder progress for long. Merchants reduced swollen inventories with special "Distress Sales!" and one enterprising Quaker, Potter Palmer, dared to plan a new, four-story, marblefront establishment on Lake Street where he would continue to permit the return of goods proved unsatisfactory, goods that he promised he would sell at below-cost prices. Although grain prices dropped from $2 to $1 a bushel, and wheat, livestock, and lumber receipts fell, and railroad earnings declined 30 per cent, the city looked ahead. Early in 1858, plans were laid for $4 million in new buildings. Work was progressing on a $10-million project to raise the streets out of the mud and also, under direction of a young engineer, George M. Pullman, to lift buildings to the new levels. In 1859, a mile of track for horse cars was laid on State Street, giving stimulus to the gradual move there of merchants and other businessmen from Lake Street. The city was crowded, shabby, and unattractive ("Half the town," reported a visitor, "was in process of elevation above the tadpole level and a considerable part on wheels"), but it would not be stilled.

In the midst of the depression, down came Mark Beaubien's old Sauganash Tavern at Lake and Market streets, to make way for a pineboard convention hall big enough for the 10,000 delegates and visitors to the Republican presidential convention in 1860. In that hall, called the Wigwam, Abraham Lincoln was nominated on May 18. He went on to win the presidency, and the prospects for a civil war grew.

When war came the following April with the bombardment of Fort Sumter, George F. Root, the city's premier popular composer, instantly penned a song whose opening lines were "The first gun is fired, may God protect the right!" Chicago responded by sending 3,000 volunteers in the first three weeks. Ultimately, out of its 170,000 people, it would furnish 20,000 men for the conflict, and as for economics, it would experience its biggest boom yet. With its water and rail transportation untouched by warfare, its location would prove crucial for the manufacture and distribution of everything essential for armies in the field. War orders swamped the town. Grain shipments in 1862 alone went from 16 million to 65 million bushels, and in that same year the city tripled the pork production of Cincinnati, once the nation's "Porkopolis." Factories of all kinds worked double and triple shifts turning out everything from reapers and steel plows, to saddles, harnesses, and metal and wood products. The business of banks grew so large that the Chicago Clearing House had to be established. Fortunes were made in old and fresh enterprises, the latter including the steel industry, begun in the 1850s and now turning out the first steel rails made in America. The times were lush and financially fruitful.

As ever, ripe prosperity brought dangers. During the war the city swarmed with criminals. "We are beset on every side by gangs of desperate villains," cried the *Tribune*. Brothels, gambling dens, and grog shops lined every street in the business district. Robberies and murders became commonplace. Nor did conditions improve at the war's end. The city's moral tone was lamentable. Political corruption was at a high, with councilmen making quick booty in deals with contractors seeking swift action for franchises to pave streets or build bridges or dig tunnels. Too many citizens who should have known better paid scant heed to occasional clean-up movements, and even less heed to those who warned of dire things to come. The emphasis was on material progress, of which there was constant evidence—from the ever-increasing network of rail lines and the "revolution" on State Street (with Marshall Field and Levi Z. Leiter as supreme successors to Potter Palmer, now heavily engaged in real estate), to the ever-expanding status of the city as the world's biggest lumber market (with ships from the upper Great Lakes jamming the harbor), and the scores of new mansions and thousands of other dwellings (almost all of

CHICAGO'S FIRST NATIONAL political convention was held in this building at Lake and Market streets in 1860. Hastily put up to house Republican delegates gathering to nominate a candidate for the presidency, it was called the Wigwam. Two days after the delegates convened on May 16, New York's William H. Seward led the first ballot with 173½ votes and Illinois' favorite-son candidate, Abraham Lincoln, was second with 102. It took three more ballots before Lincoln won the nomination, with Judge David F. Davis and the *Tribune's* Joseph Medill his foremost supporters. The roar from delegates and spectators was so deafening that a salute fired from the roof of the Wigwam could hardly be heard. (CPL)

[28]

IN THE CIVIL WAR, Chicago furnished some 20,000 men, more than ten per cent of its total population. Its idol was the dashing Col. Elmer E. Ellsworth, who organized a regiment of Zouaves, shown here receiving its colors after Ellsworth returned to his native New York to organize the New York Zouaves. The first Union officer to die in the war, Ellsworth was killed when, seeing a Confederate flag flying atop a hotel in Alexandria, Virginia, he hauled it down and was fatally wounded by the hotel manager. Throughout the war Ellsworth's Zouaves were in great demand to train Union troops. (CPL)

them ,violating regulations against excessive use of wood) that had gone up to house the hordes of residents that by the end of the decade numbered close to 300,000, nearly three times as many as had lived there in 1860.

And then: the Great Fire.

In the first week of October 1871, more than thirty fires sprang up in this "city of wood," the last one on the night of Saturday the seventh wiping out four blocks and causing $750,000 in damages. The next night, a small fire started in the barn behind the frame home of Patrick and Catherine O'Leary on De Koven Street, a muddy tract in a neighborhood of Irish working folk around Halsted and 12th streets.

Even now, after all these years of retelling that tragedy, arguments can be stirred about whether Mrs. O'Leary's cow touched off the fire by kicking over a lighted lantern, but such dispute dims in consideration of what those sparks in the hay-filled stable caused.

The flames roared swiftly over the crowded city, toward the east and the north. Whipped by self-generating winds, they were not daunted for some twenty-nine hours. Grand hotels, banks, churches, and schools, business houses, stores, mansions, and rail terminals, hovels, official edifices, jails, theaters, docks, and brothels—all, and more, vanished in turbulent flames. When it was over, the Great Fire had wiped out nearly $200 million in property. In all, 17,500 structures lay in ruins and ashes, and more than 100,000 were homeless. The known dead, by body count, numbered 120, with as many as three hundred more whose bodies were never recovered. There were acts of heroism and valor and craven ones, too, and many a millionaire was transformed into a pauper within blazing minutes.

The proud and braggart city that had preened itself only recently in the words of local rhymester Will Carleton, on being "the rich and voluptuous city, the beauty-thronged, mansion-decked city, the golden-crowned . . . Queen of the North and the West," contemplated the desolation and the wreckage.

And it now faced the greatest challenge of its young lifetime.

ON THE SOUTH SIDE since 1862, Camp Douglas (named for Stephen A. Douglas, who had died the previous year), was a prison for captured Confederate soldiers, of whom some are shown here. After Union triumphs at Fort Donelson that February 16, some 7,000 were jammed into the camp, striking fear into many Chicagoans but spurring anti-Union plotters into a plan to free them and take over the city. With the aid of Thomas Hines, a Confederate agent, and local sympathizers and members of the Sons of Liberty, just before presidential election day in November 1864, bands of zealots began streaming into town. The camp's commandant, Col. Benjamin J. Sweet, swiftly thwarted the massive plot by sending several detachments to arrest the leaders, including former mayor Buckner S. Morris, and seizing munitions in the home of a wealthy contractor, Charles Walsh. Before the war's end, many prisoners of the camp died of typhoid, and those not returned to their home towns lie buried in Oakwoods Cemetery. (KC)

CHICAGO'S JOY over the end of the Civil War was short-lived when on the morning of April 15, 1865, news came of the assassination of President Lincoln. Every business house closed, including saloons. The body of the martyred president was taken to Springfield for burial, and on the way the funeral party paused in Chicago. While the black-draped Illinois Central train waited on the lakefront tracks, the casket was carried to the courthouse, escorted by nearly 50,000. On May 2, the president lay in state in the courthouse, where, as seen in this rare photograph, 130,000 citizens came to pay their respects through the day and night. (KC)

[30]

A SOURCE OF AFFLUENCE during the Civil War was livestock transported by rail for slaughtering in small plants and makeshift abbatoirs. There had long been a clamor for centralization of all facilities involved and, on Christmas Day 1865, the stock yards came into being on 345 acres centered around Halsted and 39th streets, and known officially as the Union Stock Yard and Transit Company. Most of its $1-million capitalization was furnished by railways, the rest by packers. The yards were then the most modern in the land, able to accommodate more than 100,000 head of cattle and hogs. This is believed to be the first photograph of the yards, taken by a French newspaper editor. (KC)

JUST BEFORE THE GREAT FIRE, Theodore R. Davis meticulously spotted nearly fifty buildings, railroad stations, bridges, tunnels, parks, and other points of interest in this *Harper's Weekly* panoramic drawing of Chicago. When he was doing the research and preliminary sketches, Chicago was a city of 334,000 and still something of a wood-structured frontier town, six miles long and three miles wide. It contained extremes of wealth and squalor, from Terrace Row on South Michigan Avenue, to Conley's Patch a few blocks to the west, and seemed constantly beset by fires. In 1870 alone, there were six hundred, most starting by lighted lamps overturning in barns. An ordinance forbade the use of uncovered lamps near hay or straw but, with typical irreverence, Chicagoans paid it no heed. (FNB)

ONE ARTIST'S VERSION of how the Great Chicago Fire began on the Sunday night of October 8, 1871: The traditional account is that Catherine O'Leary went into the barn behind the frame house she occupied with her husband Patrick and their children on De Koven Street to get milk for some punch and that the cow kicked over a lantern, setting fire to nearby hay. This is more or less the story Mrs. O'Leary told an insurance investigator the next morning, but subsequently she changed it several times, obviously fearful that anti-Irish mobs might descend in vengeance on the neighborhood. Other contemporary depictions showed Mrs. O'Leary as a witch, a harridan, and a drunken slattern. Whatever the cause, the fire did begin in that barn, did spread with extreme rapidity—mainly because of delays in sending hard-pressed firemen to the correct location—and could not be halted for twenty-nine consecutive hours. (KC)

[32]

A LURID CONCEPTION of Chicago in flames, one of many hundreds made by artists who were rushed to the scene by out-of-town newspapers and magazines: No photograph exists that might have been taken during the fire, unless it was perhaps destroyed in the holocaust, or lost in the crowd pushing and shoving toward Lake Michigan, "the blessed lake shore." (KC)

THE COURTHOUSE-CITY HALL downtown at Randolph and Clark streets was ravaged beyond saving, as shown here in a view of it behind the ruins of another building. It had been a magnet for the fleeing crowds, but a few hours after the fire started its roof was already smoldering, as in the drawing below. The bell in its tower clanged constantly until about 2 a.m. on October 9, when the tower collapsed along with the roof. Prisoners lodged in the basement cells had already been marched out or had escaped. A real estate agent, John G. Shortall, and a friend performed an invaluable service by grabbing a wagon at gunpoint and cramming it with whatever vital records they could salvage before the interior was a mass of flames. (KC-CAM)

[33]

FLAMES STILL COURSE through the city while this weary band sits disconsolately in a sheltered area. Thousands of others took refuge in Lincoln Park, a former cemetery designated a park only two years earlier, and many wandered westward to the safe prairies before the flames reached the city's North Side after leaping across the Chicago River. In all 100,000 were made homeless, and tents and quickly built barracks were pressed into use. Many charitable deeds were recorded, but some grocers doubled prices on such scarce commodities as bread, cheese, and milk, while fresh water sold for $5 a barrel. (CPL)

CHICAGO'S MAYOR, Roswell B. Mason, tried during the Great Fire to control the panic-stricken hordes, thieves, and looters by proclamation and exhortation. A civil engineer who had overseen the five-year construction of the Illinois Central Railroad, he had been elected in 1869, and was nearing the end of his two-year term when the city was stricken. In addition to ordering the closing of saloons and warning robbers, Mayor Mason sought to soothe the situation by this kind of public statement late in the fire's second day: "It is believed that the fire has spent its force and all will soon be well." When the fire had indeed spent its force, he declared martial law and put Gen. Philip H. Sheridan of Civil War fame in charge of experienced army veterans and raw volunteers. This created a considerable controversy with Gov. John Palmer that ended after a young recruit accidentally shot the city prosecutor to death for not heeding a command to halt. (KC)

"RUINS! RUINS! Far and wide from the river and lake to the prairie side!" went a song written by George F. Root hours after the Great Fire, and this view on the morning of October 10, looking north and west from Wabash and Congress streets, verifies that sad lyric. That inveterate booster, John Stephen Wright, stood at this very corner on that dismal morning, staring at the ruins, when D. F. Horton, publisher of Wright's book, *Chicago Past, Present and Future* some years earlier, came by and asked, "Well, Wright, what do you think now of the future of Chicago?" Wright replied, "I will tell you what it is. Chicago will have more men, more money and more business within five years than she would have had without the fire." Wright's optimism was mirrored in the words of other boosters, notably William "Deacon" Bross, a newspaper editor and civic leader who sped to the East to tell audiences: "I tell you that within five years Chicago's business houses will be rebuilt and by the year 1900 Chicago will boast a million souls! Go to Chicago now!" (CHS)

From Calamity to Celebration: 1872 to 1893

NOTHING IN CHICAGO'S HISTORY more memorably exemplifies its ability to survive catastrophes small or large than its resurgence after the Great Fire. Rival cities were quick to call it forever doomed, some of them likening its fate to that of Sodom and Gomorrah. But they and other nay-sayers were grievously wrong. The local Boosters and Boomers were tireless in seeking ample credit from Eastern banks and capitalists with interests in the stricken city. Financial help came from all over the country and from Europe—$5 million in funds, food, and clothing. Of immense importance was the survival of the Union Stock Yards, the docks and outlying railroad tracks, and the scores of factories that lay outside the scope of the flames. And the Queen of the West endured.

Debris was cleared away while some sections still smoldered. Refugees were cared for in dozens of shelters and aid stations. Hundreds of temporary homes were clapped together, and solid rebuilding also began. The city pulsated with activity. Indeed, within three years after the Great Fire, impressed visitors called Chicago "the marvel of the age," and a magazine writer spoke for many: "This is a peerless metropolis in its indomitability of spirit, in its solidity of structure, in its imposing architecture, in its development of a sleepless vitality, an unaltering faith and an irrepressible progressive impulse."

In the post-fire decade there were problems aplenty, ranging from violations of building-safety ordinances and a rise in criminality, to financial panic and conflicts between workers seeking better wages and conditions and stubborn industrialists repelling what they considered "radical" demands. But the city maintained its frenetic pace, continuing to thrive and expand its status as the nation's major center for shipments of grain, livestock, and lumber. Sarah Bernhardt, on her first visit, performed for adoring theater crowds, visited the Union Stock Yards ("a dreadful and magnificent sight"), and paid the city compliments ("Chicago is the pulse of America, I adore it"), offering also perceptive comment about the go-getting aspects of all around her: "It is a city in which men pass each other without ever stopping, with knitted brows, with one thought in mind—the end to attain."

There was innovation in the city of a lasting sort. One of the basic results of the Great Fire was a need to reexamine the designs of many of the fallen buildings in order to devise better, safer ones. There were young architects who, in the wake of disaster, were ready for experiments in new ways, and out of what they did grew the city's great architectural age, beginning in the mid-1880s. The fame of the new structures spread, bringing a pleasure to the civic-minded that obscured less admirable aspects of the period, such as the horrors of a Haymarket Square bombing and the subsequent trial so fraught with passion and prejudice.

For all its undoubted accomplishments since the holocaust of 1871—social, cultural, educational, and material—Chicago seemed to older, more venerable cities an audacious youngster when it dared to bid for the multi-million-dollar exposition that Congress authorized in 1889 to celebrate the 400th anniversary of Columbus' discovery of America. But the backers of the application were a determined lot, arguing intensely with glowing promises. The city won the right to stage the mammoth fair, and a new era was at hand.

THE VERY FIRST to erect a building in the devasted business district was a young real estate dealer named William D. Kerfoot. On Washington Street between Clark and Dearborn streets he and some friends put up a crude wooden shack, twelve by sixteen feet, and on it he affixed a hastily lettered sign that became part of the post-fire lore: "ALL GONE BUT WIFE, CHILDREN AND ENERGY." Within days, he had to expand his quarters and make room for a firm of lawyers and a team of surveyors, all shown below. (KC)

"CHEER UP" was the heading on a *Tribune* editorial shortly after the fire, and it ended with
"Chicago shall rise again!" This soon was exemplified in hundreds of places as the city started to re-
cover. A city hall was an immediate imperative, and one was hastily knocked together early in 1872
around a rusting, empty water tank at La Salle and Adams streets. It would be the seat of city government until 1885. The tank itself was pressed into service as the city's first free public library, with
some 7,000 volumes donated by many countries—mainly Great Britain, whose donors were led by
Queen Victoria and included Benjamin Disraeli, John Stuart Mill, and Dante Gabriel Rossetti.
(KC-CAM)

THREE DAYS AFTER the Great Fire, the Board of Trade passed a resolution urging the rebuilding of its home, the old Chamber of Commerce building. On November 6, the cornerstone was laid, and there was a rush to complete it. Beyond this maze of posts, ladders, and scaffolding at Washington and La Salle streets, workmen can be seen finishing the roof. It was ready on the following October 9, a day marked with band music, oratory, and a parade. Another impressive newcomer in 1872 was the depot shared by the Lake Shore & Michigan Southern and the Chicago, Rock Island & Pacific railways. Although many of the railroad stations had been destroyed, one fortunate aspect was that most trunk lines were still intact, an obvious stimulus toward resurgence. By the time these two buildings were finished they had joined scores of others large and small. In one year, statisticians reported, $34 million in construction had been accomplished on the South Side, $3.9 million on the North Side, and nearly $2 million on the West Side. (CHS-KC)

IN 1873, despite a financial panic that gripped the country, $30 million was put into theaters, railroad stations, banks, office buildings, and mansions. Emblematic of the recovery was this Interstate Industrial Exposition building on the east side of Michigan Avenue at Adams Street, first projected in 1871 by a business group including Potter Palmer, Cyrus Hall McCormick, and plumbing manufacturer R. T. Crane. It was opened in the summer of 1873, and for two decades it staged an annual fair designed to prove Chicago's and the Midwest's material gain. Innumerable other events there ranged from political meetings to productions by visiting opera troupes and symphony orchestra concerts. (CAM) [39]

FIRST AMONG the palatial hotels quickly rebuilt was the Grand Pacific Hotel, scheduled to have had its grand opening the night the Great Fire struck; it went up by the end of 1872 at Clark and Jackson streets, and would soon welcome among its guests the King of the Sandwich Islands. (KC)

THE GRANDEST OF THE GRAND was the new Palmer House, constructed as before at State and Monroe streets, at a cost of $3.5 million. John van Osdel, its architect, had drawn plans and sketches for it before the Great Fire. As flames neared the old hotel, he covered his documents with sand and a layer of damp clay in a pit in the basement. Afterward, he recovered them unharmed, a discovery that later led to use of clay tile for fireproofing. Among the new hotel's many awe-inspiring attractions was its barbershop *(below, center)* inlaid with silver dollars, the 25-foot-high rotunda *(below, bottom)*, plus several dining rooms that served such rarities as boned quail in plumage, and partridge, buffalo, and antelope steaks. (FT)

AN IMPORTANT CHICAGOAN of the 1870s was Myra Bradwell *(right)*, editor and publisher of the *Legal News,* in whose columns she constantly fought for women's rights and higher standards for the legal profession. After she was rebuffed in efforts to practice law—first because she was married, then merely because she was a woman—she kept up her fight and got a bill through the Illinois Legislature, providing that one's sex could not bar one from the professions or other employment. In June 1873, Mrs. Bradwell's protegee, Alta M. Hulett *(below),* thereupon became the first woman admitted to the bar, though she was only 19. Mrs. Bradwell's editorials were also a factor in formation in 1874 of the Chicago Bar Association, comprising forty-two lawyers. (CBA)

A. MONTGOMERY WARD, once a young clerk in the store owned by Marshall Field and Levi Z. Leiter, had a revolutionary idea in 1872. In the encircled, top-floor room of this Turnverein Hall on Clark Street north of Chicago Avenue he compiled an eight-page mail-order catalog of merchandise with his partner, George R. Thorne. His starting capital was only $2,400, but he became a millionaire many times over. His was the first such firm in the country, with Sears Roebuck and Company coming along nearly twenty years later to constitute the "Big Two" of mail-order selling. Ward also became known as the Watchdog of the Lake Front because of his incessant battle to keep the area along Lake Michigan free of structures. (KC)

[41]

THE FINANCIAL PANIC that started in 1873 set off a series of strikes and violence that lasted through 1877. In that humid summer thousands of railroad workers struck, angry over wage cuts. There were bloody confrontations between strikers and troops fresh from the Indian wars, most of them near the Halsted Street viaduct, as in this contemporary sketch. In a single July week, thirteen were killed, the loss in livestock and produce was set at nearly $3 million, and a pattern of strife between labor and capital had been firmly and bloodily established. (CPL)

THROUGHOUT MOST OF THE 1880s, Chicago's mayor was native-Kentuckian Carter Henry Harrison, a fervent booster of the city he had adopted in 1855 and a supporter of the fledgling labor unions. He pushed hard for civic progress, yet vice flourished with minimal interference. Vastly popular with the masses, he was hailed as the "Eagle" and "Our Carter." He enjoyed riding around town on his chestnut brown horse, waving his slouch hat or dismounting to discuss with citizens issues or problems of the day. Most of the newspapers steadily opposed him after his election in 1879 for the first of five terms, but even they and his political foes had to admit that he was honest and effective, despite steady support from the city's gambling czar, Michael Cassius "King Mike" McDonald. (CST)

MAYOR HARRISON liked to brag about how his city's streets were lined with business houses and constantly teemed with humanity, and this view of Clark Street looking south from Randolph Street certainly bears him out. It is 1880 and those horse-drawn streetcars are nearing their final days. (FEA)

MAYOR HARRISON'S CHICAGO was a place where one could eat well. Prominent among many choice restaurants was Chapin and Gore's *(below),* originally in Theater Alley behind the McVicker's on Randolph Street. It barred women, but was patronized by the city's wealthiest, the architects and industrialists, to say nothing of such out-of-towners as varied as "Buffalo Bill" Cody and the noted actor, Joseph Jefferson. Kinsley's *(right),* with five stories of Moorish style, not only welcomed women, but had a German restaurant, a French cafe, a Ladies-and-Gentlemen's Restaurant, an all-male buffet, and a top-floor ballroom. It liked to think of itself as the "Delmonico's of the West." Other notable eating places of the period included the Boston Oyster House, Rector's, and Billy Boyle's Chop House. (CAM-WKC)

[43]

THE FIRST CABLE CARS were into operation in 1882 by a company organized by Charles Tyson Yerkes, who would develop a reputation before the end of the century as a rapacious traction magnate and a manipulator of aldermen and state legislators. The one at left, typical of these replacements for horse-drawn vehicles, was capable of speeds up to fourteen miles an hour. What's more, cars could be leased by clubs and organizations to transport them to picnics, as these bravos *(below)* of Yerkes' Chicago City Railway Company have done. (CTA)

ANOTHER INNOVATION in the city, and the first of its kind in the world, was the use of the telephone in police patrol boxes, two years after the first telephone exchange was established in 1878. As this artist's version shows, the box seen behind the robber and his two captors was just large enough to hold one man and often served as a temporary jail until the patrol wagon rattled up. According to the *Scientific American* in a contemporary interview with a sergeant, some patrolmen found the box convenient for a nap, piling up cedar paving blocks on the floor for an easy chair. (IBT)

BOY OPERATORS handled telephone calls in those early days and, because of their frisky ways, they were called "Wild Indians." Later in the decade, after the Chicago Telephone Company built its own operations building at Washington and Franklin streets, highly trained women there replaced the boys at this far more complex magneto switchboard on the seventh floor. (IBT)

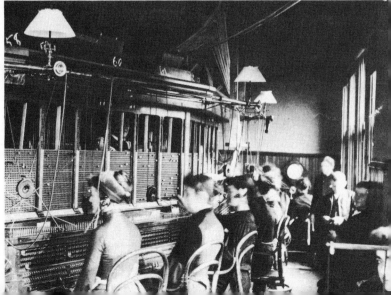

MASS MEETING

A CENTER OF STRIFE between capital and labor since the mid-1870s, Chicago was the scene of a world-stirring tragedy in 1886-87. On the drizzly night of May 4, 1886, a crowd, summoned by this circular *(facing page, top),* gathered in Haymarket Square to hear speakers denounce police brutality of the previous day outside strike-bound McCormick Harvester Works on Blue Island Avenue. Samuel Fielden, an anarchist known as "Good-natured Sam," was addressing the crowd when Police Capt. William Ward, at the head of a corps from the nearby Desplaines Street Station, ordered the listeners to disperse. "We are peaceable," replied Fielden, a second before a bomb exploded in the police ranks, killing six and wounding sixty *(facing page, bottom).* After a wide-ranging roundup, eight men headed by Albert R. Parsons *(top),* a Confederate Army veteran and an avowed anarchist, and August Spies *(above right),* fiery editor of the *Arbeiter Zeitung,* a German workers' newspaper, were tried for murder in a controversial trial. On November 12, 1887, Parsons, Spies, Adolph Fischer, and George Engel were hanged; another defendant, Louis Lingg, killed himself by swallowing dynamite; and Oscar W. Neebe, Michael Schwab, and Fielden were later pardoned by Gov. John Peter Altgeld while serving long sentences. (KC)

PEERING FROM BEHIND the masts of ships in the Chicago River at the Franklin Street Bridge is William W. Boyington's massive depot of the Chicago and North Western Railway. A close look at the cargo aboard the ships reveals evidence of the considerable lumber trade of the 1880s that came from Michigan, Wisconsin, and Canadian ports to be transported from Chicago by rail and by canal boats. The depot, built in 1881, was in use until a larger, more modern one replaced it on Madison and Canal streets in 1911. (FEA)

THE BOARD OF TRADE building, largest in the U.S., was built in 1883-85 to replace the structure that had opened a year after the Great Fire. Because the directors wanted it in the city's financial center, it was erected on Jackson Boulevard facing La Salle Street, on which banks and financial institutions would be forever concentrated. At its formal opening on April 29, 1885, invited guests came from as far away as Liverpool, England. (FEA)

TRADING HOURS in the early lifetime of the Board of Trade building, as sketched by an artist for *Harper's Weekly*: Trading in grain then, as before and since, constituted the principal function each day. It began briskly and usually closed in a frenzy, with the ringing of a gong to mark the start and finish. This was the setting for a major novel of the later Chicago literary renaissance, Frank Norris' *The Pit*. The building stood until 1929 when it was demolished to make way for its present towering successor. (KC)

[49]

WHERE ONCE STOOD the Cook County Courthouse and City Hall, in 1885 was completed John van Osdel's City Hall and County Building, as ornate, bulky, and impressive as seen here from the corner of Clark and Washington streets. Its construction, undertaken in 1877, was delayed by political bickering and occasional lack of funds. It came down in 1911 for the present building that houses many city and county offices. (CAM)

NOT ESPECIALLY IMPOSING as Chicago architecture, the Romanesque Art Institute at Michigan and Van Buren streets was important culturally. It served as an exhibition hall for both conventional art and paintings by artists then considered ultra-progressive. The institution itself, incorporated in 1879 as the Chicago Academy of Fine Arts, was an outgrowth of the highly esteemed Chicago Academy of Design, founded in 1866. A prime mover in the development of the famous organization and its president (1882-1924) was Charles Hutchinson, banker and member of a wealthy meat-packing family. The Art Institute's present, impressive home on Michigan Avenue, fronted by Edward Kemey's famous bronze lions, went up in 1893. (AI)

THE GOLDEN ERA of Chicago architecture was touched off by William Le Baron Jenney, seen here conferring with assistants in his office. One of the city's leading architects since settling there in 1867, Jenney, a former Army major, conceived the idea of constructing a fireproof building for the Home Insurance Company around a self-supporting steel skeleton, protected from fire by masonry and with beams and girders bolted together to produce a firmly united framework. In 1885, this revolutionary concept became a reality in the world's first skyscraper. It was only ten stories tall (two additional floors were added in 1911), but the building at La Salle and Monroe streets became a precedent-setting landmark in architecture. (IBT-CST)

THE ROOKERY, one of the era's glories, was the creation of John W. Root and Daniel H. Burnham in 1886 at La Salle and Adams streets, the former site of the ramshackle structure that was the City Hall and public library for several years after the Great Fire. So named because hundreds of pigeons had roosted on the eaves of its predecessor, the Rookery is one of few Chicago buildings from that period which still stand and has been declared an architectural landmark. It pioneered in providing shops and offices around a graceful semi-private square, and furthered development of Jenney's structural idea by using cast-iron columns, wrought-iron spandrel beams, and steel beams for interior support. (KC)

LOUIS HENRI SULLIVAN, the most original of the brilliant Golden Era architects, held that design should be related to utility and that architecture was a response to the milieu. He was also a devout believer in modernism and artistry's democratic traditions. He worked first in William Jenney's office, but in 1881 he and a rabbi's son, Dankmar Adler, joined forces. Their best-known creation —considered then the most famous on the continent—was the Auditorium, comprising a theater, hotel, and offices on Congress Street between Michigan and Wabash avenues. While it was a prime example of Sullivan's theories of design, the theater's remarkable acoustics were Adler's doing. On opening night, December 9, 1889, five thousand notable Chicagoans heard "Home Sweet Home" sung by Adelina Patti and speeches by Pres. Benjamin Harrison and Gov. Joseph Fifer. The Auditorium was the brainchild of a wholesale grocer, Ferdinand Whyte Peck, who got financial support from prominent industrialists and lesser citizens alike. (KC)

TWO MORE MASTERPIECES by Adler and Sullivan:
The Schiller Building—later renamed the Garrick—was
completed in 1893 on Randolph Street *(below)*, with
a theatre on the ground floor and thirteen floors of
offices. Two years later the Chicago Stock Exchange
(right) was built on La Salle Street just north of Madison
Street. Despite protests from historians and architectural
groups, both splendid structures have come down in
subsequent years, the Garrick for a parking garage and
the Stock Exchange for an office building that
experienced rental problems. (FEA)

[53]

SOME ARCHITECTS devised revolutionary office buildings and concert halls, others designed for the city's wealthy. Henry Ives Cobb built this astounding mansion for one of the richest, Potter Palmer, who startled many by hiring Cobb in 1882 for a job on a site that lay in a patch of frog ponds on Lake Shore Drive. The scoffers insisted the location was too far out, two miles or more north of the Chicago River, but Palmer outguessed them all. Within a year after he and his wife, the former Bertha Honore *(left),* moved into what came to be called Palmer's Castle, property values there went up 150 per cent. A prime element in the castle's many treasures was an art gallery, where Mrs. Palmer displayed paintings from the world over. The Palmers were easily among the city's top social leaders. In addition, Mrs. Palmer was active in committees on behalf of underpaid working girls and votes for women. (KC-CHS)

BY THE 1880s, the Palace Car Company that George M. Pullman had organized in 1867 was prospering mightily, with quarterly stock dividends of six to eight percent. Besides his sleeping cars and diners, Pullman also manufactured a parlor car *(right)*, whose innovative features by 1889 in-electric lights, fans, and steam heat. Advertisements of the day played up the luxurious aspects of the sleeping cars ("Service first-class in every respect"), as in the one below for the Chicago and Atlantic Railway's New York-to-Chicago run. (KC-WKC)

FIVE TIMES BETWEEN 1880 and 1890 the Chicago White Stockings, led by Adrian "Cap" Anson, won the National League championship. Chicago was crazy about its heroes. Editorialists criticized "baseball maniacs" who left work to troop out to White Stockings Park around Congress and Throop streets to pay their fifty cents, but the fans paid scant heed. Anson is in the center of this photograph, flanked by some of his stars after they returned in April 1889 from a tour of five continents and ten countries as part of an All-American team. The following year, a player's revolt led to formation of a new team composed mainly of beginners; fans called it "Anson's Colts" at first, and later the "Cubs." (CHS)

WHEN THE WHITE STOCKINGS were out of town, their park was used for other purposes. This is Joseph Boggs Beale's illustration of the first annual competition in 1885 of the National Archery Association. (CHS)

PERHAPS EVEN MORE POPULAR, with those who could afford to patronize it, was the Washington Park Race Track, scene of the first American Derby in 1884, won by Modesto. As is evident in this contemporary photograph, many of the patrons came in gleaming carriages and in gayest raiment, often sauntering in processions down Michigan Avenue. Before it moved to the suburbs in 1908, the South Side track was the city's most elegant, drawing gamblers and society folk alike. (WKC)

CYCLING, as a competitive sport and for recreation, was a local as well as national craze. The dapper fellow posing in Washington Park with the two glowering ladies exemplified many thousands for whom bicycling meant fun—although they annoyed drivers and passengers in carriages as they swarmed through streets and boulevards on what the *Times* described as "outlandish machines." (KC)

FOR ENTERTAINMENT less sports-oriented there was a visit to Libby Prison. Transported stone by stone from Richmond, Virginia, by the suggestion and financial support of Charles F. Gunther, an alderman and wealthy candy-maker, it was rebuilt in 1888 on Wabash Avenue south of Twelfth Street. It was a well-patronized war museum until 1911 when it was replaced by the Coliseum. Its facade was incorporated into the new building, soon the site of political conventions, civic celebrations, concerts, and assorted mass meetings. (CAM)

[58] TWENTY DAILY and weekly newspapers in this period employed scores of reporters and editors who not only covered the news, but formed professional and social organizations. An interesting one established in 1889 "for the cultivation of good fellowship" was the Whitechapel Club, with quarters in the rear of a saloon on a short street known as Newspaper Alley. Liquor flowed easily, conversation was witty and uninhibited, and the furnishings included skulls and two full-sized skeletons. Among its members were Finley Peter Dunne (left), creator of "Mr. Dooley," a satirical commentator on current affairs in the city, state, and nation; the editor-poet Wallace Rice (fifth from left); and Brand Whitlock (to the left of Rice), a young reporter then and, later, an important diplomat. The membership also included such bright journalistic memorables as Opie Read, John T. McCutcheon, Eugene Field, and George Ade. (CAM)

A VITAL AND BENEFICIAL institution was born in September 1889, when Jane Addams and Ellen Gates Starr rented rooms in this dilapidated mansion built in 1856 by Charles J. Hull on Halsted Street near Polk Street. Spurred by a summer visit to Toynbee Hall, England's pioneering settlement house, their aim was to render humanitarian and civic service to the poor in the surrounding slums. Miss Addams named the establishment Hull House and, in the years that followed, expanded its staff and its size, with twelve additional buildings. The innumerable varied programs that developed—ranging from bathing babies to teaching crafts to solving domestic problems—had deep influence on the social reform movement in America. Miss Addams, seen below in a rare photograph at the time she founded Hull House, also took active part in progressive politics in the city and worldwide campaigns against war and against racial and sexual discrimination. She won the Nobel Peace Prize in 1931, four years before her death. (JAMC)

THE HUSTLE AND BUSTLE of the 1890s all over the business district was nowhere more clearly evident than on State Street, the central shopping thoroughfare. The first view is at its intersection with Madison Street *(facing page),* soon to be labeled by civic boosters "the world's busiest corner." The second *(above)* is of the street itself looking north from Madison Street. The building under construction is the 21-story Masonic Temple which, when completed in 1892, was one of the tallest and handsomest of the growing number of skyscrapers. It came down in 1939. (CTA-FEA)

[62]

TWO MORE SCENES in the central area of the 1890s: The first is of Dearborn Street looking north of Washington Street *(facing page)*. Then, as in pre-1871 years, Dearborn was the main locale for real estate firms. Above is Randolph Street west from the Wabash Avenue elevated-train structure. The "high line" arrived in 1892 and, by 1897, the crowded rectangle between Wabash, Lake, Wells, and Van Buren streets came to be called the Loop because it was bounded by a steel band of elevated tracks upon which trains from other parts of the city converged. In a short time the Loop also included the busy commercial section that lay on the edges of as well as inside of the tracks. (KC-CHS)

THE RUSH STREET BRIDGE over the Chicago River was from the beginning a crucial passageway from the south to the north of the city and always crowded with traffic. By the last decade of the century it was said to be the busiest bridge in the world. At the left of this graphic picture, the William M. Hoyt building stands on the site of Fort Dearborn. (WKC)

[64]

THE PRINCIPAL CENTER for wholesalers of produce since the city's earliest years was South Water Street. This scene in 1892 is relatively placid, but at its busiest hours there was a kind of pandemonium, with sidewalks packed with barrels and boxes, people pushing through the clutter, and hundreds of horse-drawn wagons jamming the curbs. (KC)

SOUTH SIDE SCENES OF THE 1890s: Michigan Avenue, shown above on a Sunday afternoon with carriages gently coursing along near Thirty-fourth Street, was a kind of civic showplace where some of the second-level elite maintained mansions slightly less grand than those of Marshall Field, George Pullman, or Philip Armour on Prairie Avenue. Not far away on Vincennes Avenue between Thirty-seventh and Thirty-eighth streets was the equally fashionable Aldine Square *(below),* with graystone residences surrounding three sides of a park in whose center was an artificial lake. And in considerable contrast was Lake Park Avenue at Fifty-fifth Street *(right),* with its corner saloon euphemistically characterized by its owner Charlie Friedrich as a "family resort." (KC-CDN-IC)

CHICAGOANS YEARNING FOR the "better things" found part of their wishes fulfilled when Theodore Thomas became conductor of its new symphony orchestra in 1891. Thomas, a brilliant German-born musician, had visited the city with various orchestras since 1869, but with this appointment by the Orchestral Association he was here for good, forming one of the nation's best orchestras by the time he died in 1905. He was always totally absorbed in his musical career: "I do not work for money or business. I work only for art." And he was eternally a local booster: Told of a musician who had died heartbroken, he said, "Poor fellow, he had no Chicago to go to." (CDN)

SYMBOLIC of A. Montgomery Ward's long and persistent battle to keep the lake front free of encumbrances (he made an exception for the Art Institute) is this 1892 view of the city's downtown harbor in Grant Park as seen from atop the Kimball Building at Jackson Boulevard and Wabash Avenue. With opening day of the World's Columbian Exposition approaching in 1893, many land developers and promoters sought to overthrow the Ward-sponsored ordinance, but Ward fought them all off at considerable cost in legal battles. (CST)

Triumphs and Tumults: 1893 to 1920

THE MANIFOLD WONDERS of the "White City," as the sparkling collection of buildings and vast attractions of the World's Columbian Exposition came to be known on every continent, drew visitors from all over the world—27,500,000 in all, from opening day at the beginning of May to the end of October in 1893.

The largest crowds streamed in from the farms, small towns, and villages of the Midwest, and scores returned afterward to settle in the city of which the entire world, for better or worse, seemed to be taking note. Then, slowly at first but soon in a flood after the advent of the twentieth century, came increased numbers of European immigrants. Many went to work for menial wages, settling in ethnic clusters that gave Chicago a distinctive character it would retain for a long time. Already it housed more Scandinavians and Dutch than any other American city, and now it also had the largest concentrations of Poles, Lithuanians, Bohemians, Croatians, and Greeks.

In the wake of the massive fair a deep depression befell the city: thousands starved, thousands more were jobless. Once again, strife between labor and capital intensified. Vice districts flourished, and so did crime. "You are gigantic in your virtues," cried a British editor, William T. Stead, to civic leaders, "and gigantic in your vices. I don't know in which you glory most." Concerned men and women responded by forming organizations whose first aim was to improve economic conditions, but when this proved to be too complex an undertaking they concentrated on cleaning up political corruption, principally in the City Council where thieving aldermen sold franchises and favors to unscrupulous business moguls the way that butchers sold sausages over meat counters.

Another outcome of the World's Columbian Exposition was a desire by commercial leaders—and aesthetic-minded citizens—to emulate what they considered the fair's beauty in Jackson Park by improving the look of the murky, ugly city to the north of it. Out of this came new parks and playgrounds and, most importantly in 1909, the comprehensive Chicago Plan for the city's physical and cultural improvement. By this time there were various residential changes; the wealthy had moved from elite Prairie Avenue to the "Gold Coast" on Lake Shore Drive, and their houses and others nearby were cut up into small apartments while, nearby, a "Black Belt" broadened and lengthened as thousands of blacks came up from the South to join the work force.

The First World War, with a former cowboy named William Hale "Big Bill" Thompson in the mayor's chair, found the city initially divided. Thompson was so rabidly anti-British that until the country's entry into the conflict he was denounced as pro-German by patriotic groups and political foes. For all the lingering animosities, Chicago was among the leaders in subscriptions to Liberty Loans for a total of $772 million.

There was a kind of hectic wartime prosperity. Packinghouses worked their men—and women—overtime, and factories began turning out shells, barbed wire, uniforms, and gas masks. The epidemic of construction that had started in the late 1880s and gone on year after year slowed down because of war demands, but the Chicago Plan had not been shunted aside. There was now a Chicago Plan Commission to put its proposals and projects into effect. With the war ended—and with Thompson now yearning to change his wartime sobriquet of "Kaiser Bill" to "Big Bill the Builder" as he returned for a second term in 1919—the time was ripe for a renewal of such citywide activity.

IN 1893, AFTER OUTBIDDING older and richer cities, Chicago staged the multimillion-dollar World's Columbian Exposition to mark the 400th anniversary of the discovery of America. During the several years' competition for the right to hold the exposition, the city acquired one of its lasting nicknames: Charles Dana in his *New York Sun,* commenting on the promises of the Midwest upstart, editorialized, "Don't pay any attention to the nonsensical claims of that windy city. Its people couldn't build a world's fair even if they won it." A committee of 6,000, largest in the history of any such similar venture, handled every detail, and although the official observance date in 1892 passed without an opening, on May 1, 1893, the White City was finished. All the main streets were bedecked with flags, and crowds jammed downtown on their way to trains and cable cars that would transport them to the vast expanse of buildings constructed over some six hundred acres of near-swampland in what had been the South Side's half-finished Jackson Park. (CAM)

FOR ALL VISITORS to the fair, the first of scores of impressive sights was the Administration Building, Richard Morton Hunt's creation, and the surrounding pavilions, bridges, and broad avenues leading to it. The work of the many first-rank architects recruited by Daniel Burnham, chief of construction, and including Hunt, Sullivan, Adler, Root, Solon H. Beman, and Henry Ives Cobb, had a heavy influence on contemporary and subsequent architecture and gave new emphasis to white classicism, submerging the elaborate Romanesque and Victorian Gothic. Sullivan's Transportation Building was clean and stark, however, compared with the others and a favorite with European experts, who called it "appropriately modern and cyclonic." (JA)

A STRIKING SIGHT from the west end of the exposition: On the left across the basin are the Agricultural Building and Machinery Hall, and on the right is the elaborately fashioned McMonnies Fountain. Hundreds of journalists came to record the sights, and one was a young reporter named Theodore Dreiser. "All at once and out of nothing," he wrote, "in this dingy city . . . which but a few years before had been a wilderness of wet grass and mud flats, and by this lake which but a hundred years before was a lone silent waste, has now reared this vast and harmonious collection of perfectly constructed and showy buildings, containing in their delightful interiors the artistic, the mechanical and scientific achievements of the world." (KC)

[70]

THE PALACE OF FINE ARTS was hailed by Augustus St. Gaudens, then America's foremost sculptor, as "unequaled since the Parthenon and the age of Pericles." The $750,000 edifice contained millions of dollars worth of art from all over the world. Every other structure of the exposition was not meant to be permanent, being constructed of a mixture of plaster and fiber, but the Palace of Fine Arts was solidly built and fireproofed on the insistence of some of the countries that had loaned paintings and sculpture. After the exposition it became the Field Museum of Natural History, remaining so until a new Field Museum was built in Grant Park in 1920. For a number of years the glorious old building was in disarray and decay until in the 1930s it was transformed and modernized into the Museum of Science and Industry. (MSI)

FOR ALL THE SCIENTIFIC, artistic, and cultural glories at
the great fair, the Midway Plaisance linking Washington and
Jackson parks was the mass favorite. Its visitors, whether on
foot or arriving in this formidable conveyance that touted
the White Horse Inn, could take their pick of amusements of
a hundred different kinds, from sideshows to native villages
to animal circuses to games of chance. "Come, boys, let's
away to the Midway Plaisance," sang Eugene Field in his
"Sharps and Flats" column in the *Daily News*. "There are
visions of loveliness there to behold!" (KC)

THIS ATTRACTION lured nearly two million customers that
pleasurable summer. Standing at one end of the Midway, it was
the ingenious invention of George Ferris to match the dominance
of the Eiffel Tower at the Paris Exposition of 1889. Its thirty-six
cars revolved at a leisurely pace at their topmost height of 265
feet and gave passengers a chance to see, on a clear day, as far
north as the towers of the city's new skyscrapers. (IBT)

A SENSATION of the exposition was a Syrian dancer named
Fareeda Mahzar, who billed herself as "Little Egypt" and did
the hootchy-kootchy with a dance troupe at the Streets of
Cairo. For a generation or more there would be men to vow
they had glimpsed her in the nude, wearing nothing but a
huge diamond garter. Actually, she wore a full, semi-trans-
parent skirt and a heavily tasseled brassiere—although she did
have diamonds on her garters and sharped-eyed gawkers could
sometimes catch a quick look. (KC)

CHICAGO DAY at the exposition was October 9, commemorating the Great Fire. Exceeding half the city's population, more than 750,000 persons came, in and atop cable cars, by wagon and carriage, or on foot. Among the special attractions that day was the Wild West show of "Buffalo Bill" Cody, featuring the sharpshooting Annie Oakley along with Cody, the long-haired buffalo hunter and showman. (KC)

[72]

TRAGEDY STRUCK as the great fair came to an end. On its last day, October 28, Mayor Carter Harrison was cheered and applauded at Mayor's Day ceremonies. That evening, Patrick Eugene Prendergast, whom the mayor had rejected for the post of city corporation counsel, rang the mayor's doorbell on Ashland Avenue and asked to see him. When Harrison came out to the hallway, Prendergast fired at him, fatally wounding him. Chicago mourned and, although Prendergast's lawyers (including the young Clarence Darrow) sought to prove him mentally unbalanced, Prendergast was hanged. This *Harper's Weekly* illustration depicts crowds outside the Harrison home that night and, in an inset, the killer. (CPL)

THE YEAR OF THE EXPOSITION was also one in which two First Ward politicians began nearly a half century of partnership. John "Bathhouse John" Coughlin *(right)* had been a rubber in a bathhouse, a bathhouse owner, and now Democratic alderman from the ward, a polyglot area of rich men's dwellings, slums, tenements, and the notorious Levee. Michael "Hinky Dink" Kenna was tiny, a genius for political organization, and owner of the Workingmen's Exchange, a popular saloon in which—as shown below, with Kenna third from the left—gathered politicians, pimps, gamblers, pickpockets, and brothel owners, a goodly sector of the Coughlin-Kenna organization. The "Lords of the Levee" helped madams secure protection from the police and took part in boodle payments to the City Council's "Gray Wolves" contingent. Coughlin wrote terrible poetry or recited what reporters wrote for him, wore garish clothes, and lost a fortune betting on horses. Kenna said little, chewed on cigars, and accumulated riches. Their First Ward balls at the Coliseum were for a decade riotous affairs where Levee denizens mingled with society thrill-seekers, police captains, and political leaders. (KC)

THESE POLICEMEN of the Canalport station in the mid-1890s were solemn fellows, except for the sole smiler second from the right in the top row. Newspapers incessantly called on the local police to shut down gambling and prostitution and catch criminals, but not until the summer of 1894 when the Civic Federation pressured Mayor John "Dapper Johnny" Hopkins and handed him a list of gaming places was any meaningful action taken. One criminal who gave the police immense trouble was Herman Mudgett, better known as Henry H. Holmes. He lived in a ninety-room house on Sixty-third Street where he systematically murdered so many people that no exact number could be determined; police and newspaper guesses ranged from thirty to two hundred. From 1892 until his arrest late in 1894 he not only lured and disposed of victims but planned swindles and other crimes. He was hanged on May 7, 1896, and the *Chicago Journal* spoke for many: "It is safe to assume that a sigh of relief will go up from the whole country with the knowledge that this man or monster has been exterminated—much the same as a plague to humanity would be stamped out." (CPD-KC)

STRIKES AND LABOR TROUBLES sprang up when, within a week after the World's Columbian Exposition opened, the country suffered a financial depression in the aftermath of a stock market crash. By the winter of 1893, the city's streets were filled by the jobless hunting for work. The worst problems affected those who worked for George M. Pullman, seen at right on the verge of conflict. Most of Pullman's workers lived in his model town constructed on the city's southern rim in the late 1870s. Its administration building *(below)* typified the architectural style of the town which he had named for himself, and which served as a sterling example of his benevolent industrial paternalism until woes developed when he slashed wages without reducing rents or food costs. (KC)

PULLMAN REJECTED DEMANDS of a company grievance committee that salary cuts, some as high as forty per cent, be restored even partially, and, moreover, he fired the complaining workers. When the American Railway Union led by Eugene V. Debs called a local strike, an association of railway executives who controlled some 50,000 miles of track discharged all employes who refused to switch Pullman cars. This led to more strikes and clashes between strikers and strikbreakers. In the early summer of 1894, Pres. Grover Cleveland ordered federal troops in to protect movement of mail trains and other essential transport. Above, soldiers are accompanying a meat train while strikers cry, according to observers, "To hell with the government!" Below, a company is in command of a mail train to which a Pullman car has been attached. (KC)

[76]

ENRAGED STRIKERS ripped up tracks and overturned freight cars. Eugene Debs, pictured here by a contemporary editorial cartoonist as a despot paralyzing the nation's traffic, was arrested for violating a federal court injunction forbidding him and his union to interfere with the mails, interstate commerce, and railroad operations. He was sentenced to six months, while American Federation of Labor Officials in an emergency session in Chicago ordered the strikers back to their jobs. (CPL)

IN CHICAGO HEADLINES for most of the late 1890s was Mrs. Leslie Carter, born Caroline Louise Dudley. Leslie Carter, prominent socially and president of the Chicago Dock Company, was solemn, staid, and eleven years her senior. She was sultry, sensuous, and oversexed. She filed for divorce; he filed a countersuit, charging her with multiple adulteries. Mrs. Carter, ambitious to be an actress, performed brilliantly on the witness stand, and the testimony was deemed so erotic that a minimum age limit of thirty-five was set for spectators. Carter won the suit and Mrs. Carter, who kept her married name, began a stage career under the almost Svengali-like guidance of David Belasco. One of her greatest hits was in *Zaza,* but when she brought it to Chicago, Carter, then president of the Chicago Elevated Railroad, refused to allow any posters for the show to appear, and the town was full of gossip and argument for or against either of the two. Mrs. Carter continued as a theatre star into the 1920s, but her ex-husband one day turned on the gas in his apartment and ended his life. (KC)

CHARLES DURYEA, the pioneer automobile builder, and his 1895 masterpiece, the "Buggynaut," water-cooled with a four-cycle engine and a clutched transmission with three forward speeds: In it, on Thanksgiving Day, his brother Frank won America's first auto race, sponsored by Hermann H. Kohlsaat, dynamic publisher of the *Chicago Times-Herald.* Duryea outlasted three other automatic gasoline carriages and two electric cars, making the fifty-five-mile roundtrip between Chicago's South Side and Evanston in 7 hours, 53 minutes. His prize was $2000. (MSI)

[78]

THE ILLINOIS SEVENTH REGIMENT was known as the "Fighting Irish" in the Spanish-American War of 1898. Marcus Kavanagh, later a superior court judge, was its commander. (CST)

SUBURBS MUSHROOMED in the 1890s, and to get residents there and back the railroad companies built new tracks, extended older ones, and added new runs. Here are two Illinois Central arrival-departure points—the Van Buren Street station *(above)* at the rim of Grant Park during an early afternoon lull and the Randolph Street station, much busier because it is 5:25 p.m., the height of the evening rush hour. Some suburbs had continued to maintain their independence, but in June 1899, residents in 120 square miles of towns and townships ringing Chicago voted to become part of the city. Six years earlier, two of the fastest-growing suburbs, Norwood Park and Rogers Park, and parts of Calumet had already joined the city, adding some 300,000 to the 1,300,000 population, second only to New York's. (IC)

FOLLOWING ITS ESTABLISHMENT in 1892 after its predecessor had gone bankrupt, the University of Chicago grew in size and stature. Its president, William Rainey Harper, who came from Yale, made it clear that he intended to mold a great institution: "It is the opportunity to do something new and different that appeals to me." And he did much that was new and different: He started the four-quarter system, established a university press and extension department, gathered scholars from everywhere (on his first faculty there were nine former university presidents). John D. Rockefeller was the school's prime benefactor, with an initial gift of $600,000 and eventual largesse of over $35 million. In 1903, its law school was dedicated and, here, Harper is lauding U.S. Pres. Theodore Roosevelt (seated on the left of Harper) before conferring on him an honorary Doctor of Laws degree. (KC)

THE CITY SUFFERED one of the worst tragedies in its history in 1903 while Eddie Foy, the nation's favorite comedian, was starring in *Mr. Bluebird,* an extravaganza at the "completely fireproof" Iroquois Theatre. In a Christmas-week matinee performance on December 30, a gauzy strip of drapery ignited from a sputtering light and in minutes the scenery was aflame. Foy ordered the orchestra to strike up a tune and stepped forward to cry out, "Please be quiet! There is no danger!" But then the flaming stage raiment fell to the floor, the asbestos curtain jammed halfway down, and the theater was soon roaring with flames, with men, women, and shrieking and howling children crowding for the exits, many of which were locked. Scores were burned fatally, and trampled and smothered, and the toll was terrible: 596 dead. This photograph shows mute but awful evidence of the devastation. (KC)

CRIME OF THE DECADE: Dressed in plain clothes, policemen pose during the massive search for the Car Barn Bandits, four young men from the slums—Gustav Marx, Harvey van Dine, Peter Niedemeyer, and Emil Roeski—who carried on a horrendous career of robbery and murder from the early summer of 1903 to the end of the year. Finally trapped in a hideout in the Indiana sand dunes, they shot it out with detectives and uniformed policemen, killing one and almost escaping. They were caught and tried the next January and hanged, except for Roeski who got life imprisonment. (CPPA)

THIS ARCHITECTURAL MASTODON which opened in 1905 was the Federal Building, comprising offices, courtrooms, and the post office. Designed by Henry Ives Cobb, who had also built Potter Palmer's Lake Shore Drive castle, it was the scene of many important federal trials—and also of suicides of unhappy people who leaped from interior balconies on top floors down to the ornate floor below. (CAM)

CARTER HENRY HARRISON the Younger followed in his father's steps. Elected in 1897 as a Democrat and the city's first native-mayor, he returned to office four times, until 1905 when Edward F. Dunne became the Democratic party's candidate. Dunne was an advocate of municipal ownership of all street railways and promised to punish those he called "malefactors of great wealth." His Republican foe was John M. Harlan, a distinguished lawyer, whose victory was predicted by a 30,000 plurality. But Dunne won and, as shown here, was inaugurated that April 10 in the City Council chambers; he is standing at left, with Harrison at his side. (KC)

THE HORSE, despite the coming of new transportation devices, was still doing service around town. All the city's fire engines were still pulled by such sturdy steeds as those shown here *(facing page, bottom)*. Service wagons such as this one of the Chicago Telephone Company *(above)*, whose two-man toll-line crew has paused on a muddy street to be photographed, were very much in use by utilities companies. And this royally bedecked driver *(below)* is pulling out of a Clark Street livery stable, presumably on his way in that handsome carriage to pick up his employer. (CFD-IBT-JA)

[83]

[84]
THE POLICE in the century's first decade, as before and since, were underpaid, and some were corruptible and became involved in scandals. In general, they were hard-working and diligent, and mostly Irish. Here is a morning lineup, and below is one of the last horse-drawn patrol wagons, replaced starting in 1905 by motorized units. (CPD)

THE AUTOMOBILE AGE arrives: A decade after Frank Duryea's memorable Chicago-toEvanston-to-Chicago exploit in 1895, Chicago had its first automobile club, with headquarters on Michigan Avenue at Harrison Street. Its members are ranged in front of it examining recent models while a horse-drawn carriage trundles by on the right. The horseless carriages were quickly put to varied uses: Rev. William Burley, the bearded gentleman next to his driver, traveled South Side streets in his "Gospel Automobile," not only to pause at corners for a song or two by his singer Ernest Robinson and organist Marjorie Robinson, but to advertise services at his Covenant Baptist Church. (CDN-JA)

SEARS MOTOR BUGGY

SPEEDY, ECONOMICAL, NOISELESS, DURABLE AND SAFE — A CHILD CAN RUN IT

$395.00

FOR CAR COMPLETE WITH RUBBER TIRES, TIMKEN ROLLER
BEARING AXLES, TOP, STORM FRONT, THREE OIL-BURNING
LAMPS, HORN AND ONE GALLON LUBRICATING OIL
—NOTHING TO BUY BUT GASOLINE.

ALL SPEEDS FROM 1 TO 25 MILES PER HOUR

No. 21R333   Sears Motor Buggy, complete as described below. Price...........................$395
No. 21R444   Sears Motor Runabout, without top and fenders, but otherwise as described below. Price........370
     Shipped from factory, crated so as to secure the lowest possible freight rate. Shipping weight, about 1,400 pounds.
EXTRAS IF WANTED—Acetylene Lamps with Generator in place of the two front oil burning lamps.......................

WHY WE BUILD IT AS WE DO

In designing the Sears Motor Buggy we had in mind a self propelled vehicle to take the place of the top buggy and runabout; we had in mind a substantial, well built, economical, safe durable and noiseless machine; we had in mind a maximum speed that was reasonable and fast as anybody should ride; namely, 25 miles per hour.

With these things in mind and knowing what was needed throughout the country, we set about several years ago experimenting with different automobiles. We examined all the different principles used in the construction of self propelled vehicles; we examined the most successful cars to find out what they were using in the way of tires, wheels, axles, springs, transmissions, etc. We found that all the successful high grade cars were fitted with TIMKEN ROLLER BEARING AXLES, we therefore use them on the Sears Motor Buggy; we found that for regular road work there was nothing better fitted or more durable than a Sarven's patent wheel; therefore, you will find Sarven's patent wheels on our Sears Motor Buggy. We found that a wheel about 36 inches in height was the proper height to give the road clearance necessary and to give the most satisfactory service and the least vibration. We found that there was more resiliency, more comfort and more service in a FULL ELLIP-TIC SPRING than there was in any other type of spring; we, therefore, hung our Sears Motor Buggy on four full elliptic springs. We found that all the heavy, powerful automobiles and automobile trucks were fitted with DOUBLE CHAIN DRIVE FROM THE REAR WHEELS; therefore, you will find the double chain drive on the Sears Motor Buggy. We found that the fastest cars, those that were making records for speed were built with the double chain drive. At the Automobile Show in Chicago, held in February, 1909, we noticed that the car that won the New York Paris Race was built with a double chain drive, we also noticed that the car that won the last Vanderbilt Cup for making the fastest time was built with a double chain drive. We found that there was a maker of automobile frames that was making 75 per cent of all the frames used in automobile construction in the United States. We found on account of the volume of business that this concern could make frames cheaper for automobile manufacturers than the manufacturers could make them themselves. We went to this frame maker and asked him to make a frame for our Sears Motor Buggy and then to name us prices for these frames in large quantities, the result is that the angle steel frame of the Sears Motor Buggy is built by experts who build 75 per cent of all the automobile frames used in the United States today, and so on throughout the entire construction of this Sears Motor Buggy, you will find every piece and part has been given the most careful study, you will find that the Sears Motor Buggy is made of the best possible material; it is constructed to take the place of the top buggy, it is built in our own factory under the direct supervision of our own expert, a man who has had fifteen years of automobile experience, a man who has for the past three years been working with us to develop the right car for all kinds of service, and we honestly believe that in this Sears Motor Buggy we have exactly the right car for the people, at a price within the reach of all.

There are a great many buggies with engines attached that are being offered for that are nothing more than makeshifts. No ordinary buggy is built to stand the and strain given it when machinery is attached. Our Sears Motor Buggy is designed built from the ground up to carry the engine and machinery necessary to make it run has special rubber tires, special wheels, special axles, special springs, special body; in everything is special and is much stronger than other motor buggies, and it will outwear of any other make. At the same time, while we have the strength and durability in motor buggy, we have designed it so that it is pleasing to the eye, neat and light in struction and appearance. It is not heavy or cumbersome. Whether you buy a Sears Buggy or not, we want to urge you, in your own behalf, not to purchase an ordinary spring buggy with some machinery attached, as they are not practical.

Our Sears Motor Buggy will give you the greatest amount of service with the amount of operating expense. It is comfortable, safe and durable. We have not any attempt, in designing and building this Sears Motor Buggy, at copying the automo We have made no attempt to build a high speed or a high powered car. We do not that the average man desires to go whirling through the country at 40 to 50 miles an We furnish in our Sears Motor Buggy a practical car for use every day in the year rural or city roads; a car that will climb the hills and go over any of the roads ordinarily found in any part of the United States.

We have given this Sears Motor Buggy practical road tests in different sections of country, through sand, through mud, up hill and over all kinds of roads. This car will a great deal faster than you will ever want to send it over rural roads and can maintain speed twice as fast as the usual speed regulations in the cities and towns permit.

Our price of $395.00 is for the car complete, as illustrated and described above. furnish everything, including 1 gallon of lubricating oil. You have nothing to buy you receive the car but gasoline.

For the convenience of some people who do not desire a complete car, we state in our list of prices the amount we will allow if top or fenders are not wanted; we advise, however, that you order the complete car, as sooner or later you will want the complete outfit.

TERMS

Our only terms are cash; we do not sell on installments or extend credit. Send us your order and enclose our price in the form of a post-office money order, express money order, bank draft or check. If you don't want the motor buggy now, send us $25.00 as a deposit and we will enter your order in its turn and then later on you can send us the balance when you want us to make shipment.

We ship with the understanding that each and every car is to be exactly as represented and described, and is to be made of the best material and parts obtainable for the purpose. We guarantee every car to be thoroughly tested and tried out; in fact, given road service. We guarantee that it will run through mud, sand, over ordinary city and country roads and take all reasonable hills. Our Sears Motor Buggy under test has demonstrated conclusively that it is a great hill climber, and we have taken roads and hills where regular automobiles could not follow.

A "MOTOR BUGGY" by mail order was possible soon enough, as this advertisement *(facing page)* in the 1909 Sears, Roebuck and Company catalogue trumpeted. The vehicle was meant strictly for pleasure driving, with a maximum speed of 25 miles an hour. "We do not believe that the average man desires to go whirling around the country at 40 or 50 miles an hour," read the copy. "We furnish in our Sears Motor Buggy a practical car for use every day in the year over rural and city roads." By this time, Julius Rosenwald *(right),* a former clothing manufacturer who had become associated in 1896 with the firm's founders, Richard W. Sears and Alvah C. Roebuck, was a year away from becoming its president and lifelong leader. His original investment of $25,000 eventually grew to $250 million, a substantial portion of which went into philanthropic enterprises that ranged from bettering social and educational services for blacks to relief for fellow Jews in Europe. (SR)

AS LABOR-CAPITAL STRUGGLES CONTINUED, police were often recruited to serve as guards. In this photograph, they are riding herd on a streetcar during a 1906 conflict that developed shortly after most of the cable cars were replaced by overhead electric trolley cars. Two key issues in the bitter labor controversies of this period revolved around reduction of the working day to eight hours, a principle the anarchists had espoused in the 1880s, and improvement of conditions in sweatshops and factories. (FEA)

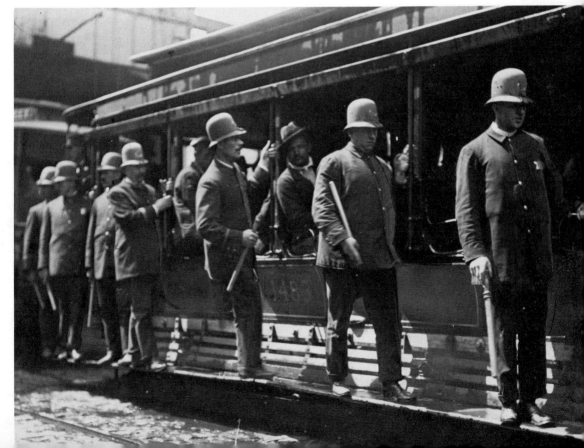

IN THE FINANCIAL PANIC of 1907, police stood on alert as gold coin was transported from the subtreasury to the First National Bank of Chicago. In this instance, six hundred sacks weighing six tons are being carried into the bank in an effort to forestall massive withdrawals. That October, important banks in other major cities failed, but the First National and most local banks remained solid. The national disaster did cause unemployment and food price increases that led to Congressional inquiries into currency and banking systems, and by 1913, the passage of the Federal Reserve Act. (FNB)

CHICAGO WAS RUSHING on its way in the early 1900s toward becoming the world's largest meat-packing center. Here, showing sheep being driven to the slaughter pens, are the expanding Union Stock Yards. (CHS)

THE MEN who brought their stock to market usually relaxed in the yards' Transit House by playing marathon games of poker. One of the muckrakers of the period, Upton Sinclair, caused a nationwide clamor with his novel *The Jungle,* which graphically described the terrible conditions in the yards and in the surrounding patches of workers' homes. This touched off governmental investigations that reported bad sanitation, dank working places, negligent inspection of meat, and other defects. Reform legislation was passed and a cleanup occurred throughout 1906. (JA)

A HAPPIER OCCASION for workingmen: These members of the Meat Cutters Union stroll along in the Labor Day Parade of 1908. The first Labor Day was decreed in New York in 1882 by Peter J. McGuire, founder of the United Brotherhood of Carpenters, to honor working people, and in 1897 it was made a national holiday. (FEA)

WHEN CHARLES COMISKEY'S "Hitless Wonders," the White Sox, won nineteen straight games in 1906 and went on to win the American League pennant, he was honored with this caricature placed alongside many others on the wall of Chapin and Gore's popular restaurant. Thousands of fans mobbed Cubs Park at Polk and Wood streets to see the "Hitless Wonders" continue their miracles by whipping the Cubs, four games to one, in the first intra-city World Series. (KC)

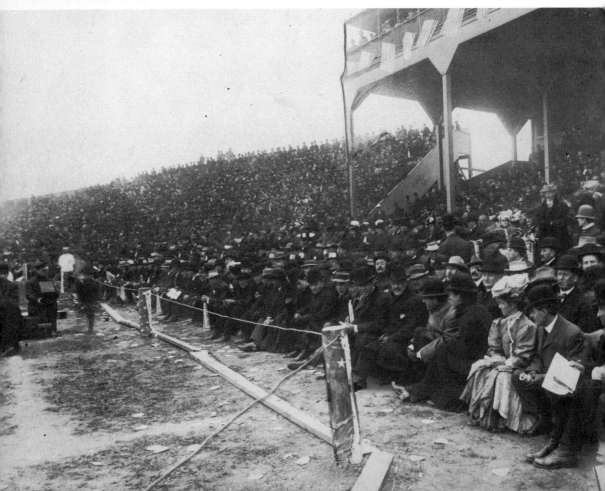

BALLOONING was a popular sport to watch and, for those daring enough, to indulge in. "Zenith" was the name of the balloon used by a daring photographer, George "Flashlight" Lawrence, to take the first of many aerial photographs of various parts of the city, including the place from which he is about to take off, the south section of the Union Stock Yards. A well-attended event in 1908 was the International Balloon Races. (WKC-CHS)

ON PLEASANT DAYS Chicagoans, as always, flocked to the parks. In Lincoln Park they could gather outside the monkey house in the zoo, a twenty-five-acre tract that often drew as many as 25,000 visitors on a warm Sunday, or they could go for a pleasant ride in the park lagoon in this swan boat. The South Side's Jackson Park was the third largest, with an eighteen-hole golf course that was the city's first public one and also these heavily patronized tennis courts. (WKC)

CHICAGO HAS always taken pride in its lakefront beaches, of which these two were typical. The one above is along the northern shore, the other in Jackson Park east of what was once the Midway Plaisance. (KC)

A MASTER ARCHITECT, Daniel H. Burnham also had a genius for city planning. In 1901, he was chairman of a commission to redevelop Washington, D.C., and later he did similar duties for Cleveland, San Francisco, and Manila. In 1905, he was asked by the Commercial Club to create a long-range plan for Chicago. In 1908, he unveiled his detailed plan, first before this group of business backers (Burnham is second from left in the upper row) that included banker Charles G. Dawes, merchants John G. Shedd and John V. Farwell, and Charles H. Wacker, vice-chairman of the newly formed Chicago Plan Commission. Burnham envisioned a City Beautiful that was also practical and pragmatic with, among other things, an unsullied lakefront, an extensive park system, a vast civic center, an improved boulevard system, the widening of such heavily traveled thoroughfares as Michigan (with a doubledecked bridge at the Chicago River), and a radial highway system in and around the city. Many of his proposals were later transformed into realities, and his famous message is embedded in the city's lore: "Make no little plans. They have no magic to stir men's blood, and probably themselves will not be realized. Make big plans. Aim high in hope and work, remembering that a noble, logical diagram once recorded will never die. . . ." (CPC)

IN THIS FERVID DECADE, Chicago certainly needed some kind of planning. This famous photograph is of an immense traffic jam at Randolph and Dearborn streets in 1909, the year Burnham's plan was published as a book and pored over by all in favor of or opposed to his suggestions. This traffic tieup was not a daily event, but the crowded conditions on South Water Street had grown worse year by year. Still the city's central depot for fruits, vegetables, fish, and poultry, it was always so busy and congested that access was sometimes immensely difficult, causing considerable food spoilage. (WKC-KC)

THE HEAVIEST INFLUX of immigrants came in the 1900s, from southeastern Europe. There were Jews fleeing persecution in Russia and Poland—120,000 in the ten years after 1900—and others came from Italy, the Scandinavian countries, and Germany. Nearly 200,000 such newcomers arrived to swell the city's population by the end of the decade to 2,185,283. These photographs are of a family in the stock yards area, and of young immigrant boys in a playground built at the urging of Jane Addams and her forceful Hull House ladies, social workers and social leaders alike. (CDN-KC)

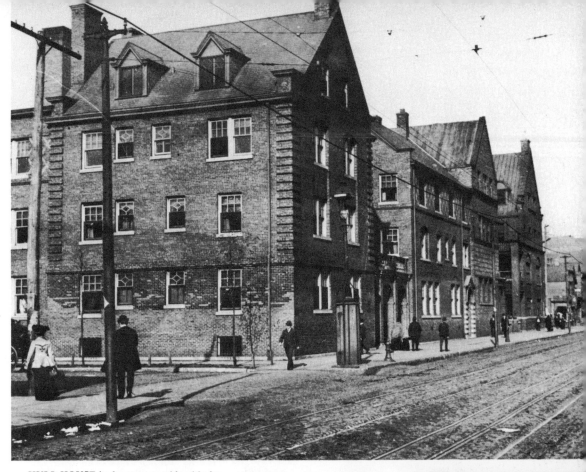

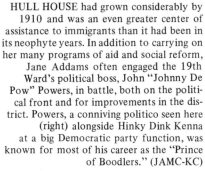

HULL HOUSE had grown considerably by 1910 and was an even greater center of assistance to immigrants than it had been in its neophyte years. In addition to carrying on her many programs of aid and social reform, Jane Addams often engaged the 19th Ward's political boss, John "Johnny De Pow" Powers, in battle, both on the political front and for improvements in the district. Powers, a conniving politico seen here (right) alongside Hinky Dink Kenna at a big Democratic party function, was known for most of his career as the "Prince of Boodlers." (JAMC-KC)

REFORMERS' CAMPAIGNS against the Levee and its denizens came to a swift climax in the second decade of the new century. For years attempts had been made by civic groups and ministerial associations to destroy the vice district. Yet in 1900 there were said to be over 10,000 prostitutes in the city, a claim that seemed to bring perverse pleasure to some who liked the concept of Chicago as a wide-open town. By then, the ruling madams were two ladies from Kentucky, Ada (or Aida) and Minna Everleigh *(left and below)*. Their Everleigh Club, an establishment that in the next ten years achieved the reputation of being the best-known bordello in the world, had a clientele that included some of the town's first citizens, to say nothing of certain visiting royalty. The Everleighs, at a price, were well protected by Kenna and Coughlin, and they eventually amassed over one million dollars, art treasures, and $30,000 in customers' IOUs. (KC)

AMONG THE REFORMERS who came to the Levee was Lucy Page Gaston, the anti-cigarette crusader. One afternoon at their club she demanded to see either of the Everleigh sisters. When Minna appeared, Lucy shrieked, "Your girls are going straight to hell! You must stop them." "What can I do?" Minna asked. "You must stop them smoking cigarettes!" shrieked Lucy. More to the point and more dramatic was Gipsy Smith, the noted evangelist. In the autumn of 1909, he led a pilgrimage of over twenty-thousand into the "Hellhole of Sin," coursed its streets of brothels—all of which, incidentally, had lowered their shades and darkened their lights—and periodically stopped in front of the Everleigh Club, the House of All Nations, and others to pray and sing hymns and such songs as "Where Is My Wandering Boy Tonight?" Ten minutes after Smith and his followers had left, the Levee lights were on again. Many marchers, making their initial visit there, stayed behind, prompting Minna to remark, "We are glad for the business, of course, but I'm sorry to see so many nice young men coming down here for the first time!" Some editorialists mocked at Smith, but nothing since William T. Stead's sulphuric expose of segregated vice in 1893, *If Christ Came to Chicago*, brought such concentrated attention on that notorious area, one result being the formation of a vice commission in 1910 that issued a voluminous report showing that commercialized vice was a $15 million-a-year business. (KC)

THE DEATH OF THE LEVEE came in 1911. It was touched off by an illustrated booklet touting the Everleigh Club and, for the first time, showing interiors such as the Blue Room *(left)*, a favorite with richer patrons, the Japanese Room *(above)*, and the Oriental Music Room *(below)*. Although the pictures were bland even by the standards of that day, and the text equally so—"Fortunate, indeed, with all the comforts of life surrounding them are the members of the Everleigh Club"—Carter Harrison the Younger, back as mayor after a six-year absence, was infuriated. The brochure, plus the blistering report of the vice commission and heightened demands from churches and reform groups, spurred him to order closing the world-famous resort forever. When the Everleigh sisters learned that not even their protectors Coughlin and Kenna could help, they retired and ended up in New York with their riches and finery, living out long placid lives like two wealthy maiden aunts. It was an end to the Levee, but most of the prostitutes, as before, dispersed to other sections of town to carry on their sought-for trade. (KC)

WILLIAM HENRY JACKSON was one of America's most famous photographers, and in 1911 he walked about the city recording many scenes. Here is the perenially busy State Street, looking south from Randolph Street, with the impressive Marshall Field and Company department store on the left. (HFM)

THE DEARBORN STREET RAILROAD STATION *(above)* with a late-model automobile in the foreground and a carriage of the Frank Parmelee Transfer System was recorded also by William Henry Jackson in 1911, as was Michigan Avenue, looking north from Congress Street, with the august Auditorium on the left. (HFM)

THE LONG BATTLE of George Wellington Streeter (forever known as Cap Streeter) versus the city's officialdom and Lake Shore Drive millionaires came to a climax in the middle of this decade. Back in the late 1880s Cap Streeter had beached his excursion boat during a storm on a sand bar in Lake Michigan between Chicago Avenue and Superior Street. Unable to free the vessel, he built a small breakwater around it and decided to stay there with his wife Ma Streeter, shown here with him. Gradually, as sand and silt settled around the boat and covered the distance from ship to shore, he proclaimed himself ruler of the "Deestrict of Lake Michigan," invited others in, sold lots, drank a lot of whiskey, and threatened to shoot anyone who dared to move him. A long series of battles ensued, and after one shooting match in which a man was wounded, Cap Streeter served nine months in the state penitentiary. When he emerged, he renewed his battle but finally, in 1918, deputies ousted him by court order and destroyed his shack. He vowed he would return to the conflict, but he was dead of pneumonia in two years. His Streeterville ultimately formed the core of a much larger area by that name which served as the site for apartment houses, skyscrapers, hospitals, the Northwestern University law school, and other buildings. (KC)

"BIG BILL," William Hale Thompson, on his election as mayor in April 1915, while his wife stands by: His victory began one of the the city's most politically raucous yet physically expansive eras. A former cowboy and athlete, Thompson was a lusty campaigner whose backers predicted he would one day be U.S. president. He assailed his Democratic foes constantly, showing the first signs of his later virulent bigotry by hinting at dire things if his opponent Robert Sweitzer, a Catholic, were elected. With lavish promises of full employment and glorious prosperity, he beat Sweitzer by nearly 140,000 votes out of 690,000, and was greeted editorially by the *Tribune* this way: "Mr. Thompson appeared on the impatient voters' horizon bulging and shining like a full dinner pail and ringing like a dinner gong." The day after election "Big Bill" bellowed, "The crooks had better move out of Chicago before I am inaugurated. . . . I want it understood that in no manner whatsoever is this to be a political machine-building administration. I am my own man!" (WKC)

AN INCREDIBLE DISASTER happened on July 24, 1915, after some 2,000 employees of the Western Electric Company joyously gathered at the Clark Street Bridge to go aboard the *Eastland,* a remodeled excursion boat, for a company outing. For reasons never determined, when all the passengers were aboard the boat suddenly listed and turned on its side. Many remarkable photographs were taken of this tragedy in which 812 persons were drowned. This one, by the *Daily News'* Fred Eckhardt, is among the most memorable. (CPPA)

CHICAGO'S MOVIE INDUSTRY sprang up early in the century when George K. Spoor and Gilbert M. Anderson (later one of the first movie cowboys, "Bronco Billy") formed the Essanay Company on the North Side and ground out two- and three-reelers every week. Their stars included Francis X. Bushman, Beverly Bayne, Ben Turpin, Wallace Berry, and Chicago-born Gloria Swanson; among their script writers was Ring Lardner. One of Essanay's rivals was the Selig Film Company, one of whose 1914 films is being made here. By 1917, Essanay was involved in complex litigation brought by independent producers against the trust of which the company was part and it collapsed. (CHS)

FITNESS PROGRAMS were in vogue and many companies instituted daily exercise routines for their employees. Here, students at the operators' school of the Chicago Telephone Company do their calisthenics atop the roof of the company's twenty-story building at Washington and Franklin streets. (IBT)

THE SANS SOUCI on Cottage Grove Avenue near Sixtieth Street might well have lasted in memory primarily as a typical amusement park with the usual array of rides and a roller skating rink except that, in 1914, its owners commissioned a combination ballroom, restaurant, and outdoor theatre. Frank Lloyd Wright, the brilliant Louis Sullivan disciple, created a masterpiece and called it Midway Gardens. The place was splendid, with structures of Cubist design, excellent band concerts, and superb cuisine. But it never caught the popular fancy, although the city's intellectuals, writers, and reporters were rather steady patrons. It all came down in 1929 for a gasoline station. (FEA)

OTHER AMUSEMENT PARKS were Riverview, up north, and White City *(below)* built at South Park Avenue and Sixty-third Street after the fashion of the World's Columbian Exposition. Eventually Riverview would outdistance White City in growth and patronage, but in these pre-World War I days White City was supreme. Among its attractions were the Barrel of Fun, the Flash, a giant roller coaster, the Chutes and, for lovers of feminine grace, performances by the girlies of the Garden Follies *(above)* (KC)

ANOTHER PLEASURE SPOT, Municipal Pier, made its debut in 1916. It stretched out into Lake Michigan with facilities for picnicking, a huge auditorium, a dance hall, three restaurants, and boats that featured good jazz-band music as they made their way from the pier to Lincoln and Jackson parks for a fee of usually not more than twenty-five cents. Its name was later changed to Navy Pier and it underwent several transformations, but it still exists today amid talk of restoring it to its first glories. (KC)

[108]

THE "GRAND OLD MAN" of the Midway was Amos Alonzo Stagg, football coach and athletic director of the University of Chicago. During the 1916 season he advised his players at practice sessions from his electric car through a megaphone because he was suffering from a severe case of rheumatism. He had come to the university the first year of Pres. William Harper's regime and molded the football team into a powerful one, with such innovations as the huddle, the shift, the man-in-motion, the end-around play, and the later-outlawed hidden-ball trick. Stagg was on the Midway for forty-one years, and before he died in 1965 at 102 he also coached at the College of the Pacific and other schools. (UC)

WORTH LOOKING AT, as these spectators outside the Sherman Hotel are doing, is this new motor-ized fire truck, one of several purchased in 1914. It would be another nine years, however, before the entire fire-fighting fleet would be mechanized and the last of the firehorses retired. Strange now, but not unusual for the time, was this elevated railroad funeral car that saw service from 1910 to 1919 *(below)*. It could be rented to take mourners to one of several cemeteries at the city's outskirts. There were specific stops along the line with elevators for caskets to be raised to the platforms, so that pall-bearers would not have to carry caskets up stairways to the train. Funeral streetcars also were available and, in the case of big funerals, extra cars could be attached. (CFD-CTA)

THE WOMAN'S SUFFRAGE MOVEMENT was strong in Chicago. When Woodrow Wilson was running for president in 1916 and showed little enthusiasm for the campaign for national suffrage, these doughty ladies expressed their views with placards and street-corner meetings—and, of course, parades. (FEA)

WHEN WORLD WAR I started in Europe, there was strong sentiment in Chicago against participation in the conflict, or even giving aid to Great Britain and France. Mayor Thompson was so vociferously opposed that pro-war editorialists labeled him "Kaiser Bill." After the sinking of the *Lusitania* in 1915, and other German acts of hostility, America entered the war in 1917, and Chicago contributed much to the war effort. In some cases, patriotic fervor was excessive: the Bismarck Hotel changed its name for the duration to the Randolph, and the Kaiserhof forever became the Atlantic. Urgent appeals were made constantly for men to enlist before they were drafted. (KC)

LIBERTY LOAN PARADES in support of the war effort, were held, such as this one passing by large crowds on the steps of the Art Institute. (KC)

CONVERTING CITIZENS into fighting men was a project that went on endlessly. Hardly a day passed, especially in the first stages of the war, without a procession of flag-bearing raw recruits heading for trains that would bear them to training camps to learn the basic elements of soldiering, and then, equipped, marching off again, some with wives and sweethearts tagging along to departure points. (KC)

THOSE MUCH TOO YOUNG to go off to battlefields, as these South Side youngsters, dug up ground on prairies and grew gardens in a nationwide program to conserve food. Throughout the city there was wartime prosperity, and production in local plants was stimulated greatly, particularly in the food-processing and metal industries. (CDN)

IT WAS ALL OVER on November 11, 1918, and troops soon started returning home, to be marched one final time down Michigan Avenue to the cheers of crowds lining the curbs and showers of flowers from pretty young ladies. (KC)

AFTER A FUTILE BID for U.S. Senator, Mayor "Big Bill" Thompson ran for relection in 1919. Once
more his Democratic opponent was Robert Sweitzer and once more Thompson won, but by a narrow
margin of 21,000 votes. "I want to make Chicago a great city, the summer resort of the United States."
he bellowed on inauguration day. "I want to build her a better lake front, to finish widening streets
and building bridges. I love this city with all my heart!" Much of his support came from districts pre-
dominated by blacks, 65,000 of whom had come from the South during the war to fill labor demands
created by as many or more departing for the armed services. Sporadic clashes between whites and
blacks climaxed in July 1919, when an assault by white toughs on black youths at the Jackson Park
beach led to five days of rioting in which 22 blacks and 16 whites were killed and 500 persons seriously
injured. An intensive study was made of the causes—social, economic and psychological—but little was
done to ease tensions, and conditions worsened as migration to the overcrowded "Black Belt" continued. (WKC)

The Years that Roared: 1920 to 1933

THERE ARE THOSE who think of Chicago of the 1920s only as that evil city of nothing but gang warfare, bootlegging and gambling and prostitution, daily carnage in the streets, theft of public funds, debasement of officials, and the operation of illegal rackets that were estimated to cost the city $136 million a year.

And Chicago was that kind of city.

Its unofficial ruler was a swarthy thug named Al Capone, who liked to think of himself as the real boss of City Hall. He supplied the wants of the many—mostly illicit liquor and whores—and gloried in it, engaging in bloody combat with rivals north, south, and west, and what he and others like him did brought shame upon the city.

Yet, it was another kind of city, too.

In that same decade Chicago boomed as it never had before. "Throw away your hammer and get a horn!" cried the cohorts of Mayor Thompson and, interestingly, there was a lot to blow horns about, from the widening of Michigan Avenue and the completion of the unique double-deck bridge over the Chicago River, to outlying street-paving projects and the creation of more parks. The physical improvements continued while "Big Bill" was out of office from 1923 to 1927. Wacker Drive, new Michigan Avenue skyscrapers, the straightening of the Chicago River, and much more gave emphasis to the words of the Chicago Plan Commission members: "Let us cease unnecessary bickering and get together. Vim and vigor lead to victory!" There were few except his colleagues in the city's literary community to pay much heed to the counsel of lawyer-poet Edgar Lee Masters that buildings and bridges alone were not sufficient to the needs of a truly great city and that "manifestly nothing can do it but the right sort of intellectual activity widely spread."

When that turbulent decade was over—and with Capone a year away from the penitentiary, having engineered in 1929 the bloodiest of all his crimes, the St. Valentine's Day Massacre—Chicago's population had soared to 3,000,000. Those buildings that Masters deplored had amounted in cost to $1 billion; there were dozens upon dozens of them, plus such impressive structures as the Field Museum and Soldier Field in the city's front yard, Grant Park. The innumerable plants and factories were making or processing $4 billion of goods annually, everything from meat products and clothing to books, machinery, and steel.

The times were gaudy, much like those in the years before the Great Fire. Sober-minded citizens paid attention to such growing vexations as the wobbly financial aspects of many of the new buildings, and the tax inequities and flagrant abuses in Thompson's administration after he was sent back for a third term in 1927. But many others reveled in the prosperity and even perversely in the iniquitous reputation. Mary Borden, a child of Chicago society and a successful novelist, returned for a visit and reflected: "No one is ashamed of anything in Chicago. Everything is moving much too quickly. Everyone is too specialized, and it is all too much fun. Each one, whether crook or politician or expert gunman, architect or banker or broker, is too good of his kind to be conscious of anything less positive and less exhilarating than his own power. . . . Everything about the big, blustering place is positive and superlative. I should as soon think of apologizing for Henry VIII or Lorenzo de Medici."

By now a new countrywide depression, touched off by the massive stock-market crash

NORTH MICHIGAN AVENUE'S development was touched off in the 1920s by completion of a massive double-decked bridge over the Chicago River between the old site of Fort Dearborn and the city's first four houses. It replaced the rickety Rush Street Bridge so many decades thronged with traffic, and required much litigation and millions of dollars in property settlements. Its design, then, was revolutionary, with traffic on two levels and hydraulic devices to raise it for vessels heading into or out of Lake Michigan. This dedication on May 14, 1920, included parades, band music, speeches, and cheers for "Big Bill" Thompson: "Hats off to our mayor! Hats off!" Later in the decade the four bridge pylons were carved with bas-reliefs denoting such historic events of the city as the voyage of Father Marquette, the Fort Dearborn Massacre, and the Great Fire of 1871. (KC)

of October 1929, had made its first effects known in Chicago. Prices of commodities dropped drastically. Soon there would be endless lines of the unemployed outside soup kitchens, and there would be payless paydays for thousands of teachers and city workers. But despite misery and woe, the city's characteristic spirit prevailed. Morris Markey, a New York magazine writer, detected it in 1932: "Millions have gathered here. They have already made Chicago the capital of the Iron Empire and a dozen other empires besides. They are intoxicated with the rush of their growth. They are determined to make of Chicago the world's largest city, the world's most beautiful city, the world's richest city, the world's most cultured city. There is not much doubt that it will dominate the stream of American civilization."

SOUTH OF THE NEW BRIDGE, Michigan had of course long been a grand thoroughfare, with the noble bronze lions of the Art Institute seemingly standing guard against any desecration of Grant Park or the lake front. Across from the institute are such venerable structures, some still standing, as the Illinois Athletic Club, the Monroe Building, The University Club, the Willoughby Building, the Tower Building topped by a massive statue of Montgomery Ward and Company's "Symbol of Progress" (Louis Sullivan scoffed that it looked like a woman in her bath), and the Chicago Public Library. North of there, the stretch from Randolph Street to the river was widened in anticipation of the big bridge's opening. (KC)

ITS NAME CHANGED from Pine Street now that the twin-decked bridge was a reality, Michigan Avenue, that would one day be known as Chicago's Magnificent Mile, stands ready in 1921 for wrecking crews and construction forces. The street has been widened and repaved, new-fangled safety islands have been installed and, although the area is still jammed with gloomy old edifices, its transformation has begun: A few blocks north of the Water Tower (center), the city's eternal symbol of survival after the Great Fire of 1871, stands the brand-new, dignified Drake Hotel, the creation of Benjamin Marshall and Charles Fox. (FEA)

IMPRESSIVE SYMBOLS of the boom on North Michigan Avenue in the 1920s were these two famous landmarks. The twin-peaked Wrigley Building (left) went up from 1921 to 1924, and offered an observatory whose twenty-five-cent admission included a package of gum made by William Wrigley's firm. Early occupants included advertising agencies, communications firms, and the Arts Club, with clubrooms and galleries and exhibits by internationally known artists. Across the street is the Tribune Tower, completed in 1925 after architects world wide had submitted entries in a highly publicized $50,000 contest that was won by Raymond M. Hood, with the famed Finnish architect Eliel Saarinen placing second. Inlaid in the floor are the words of John Ruskin, "Therefore when we build, let us think that we build forever," and imbedded in its Gothic exterior are stone fragments from celebrated buildings. (KC)

Preceeding page: COMPLETED LATE IN 1926, the $20 million Wacker Drive extended nearly a mile along the right bank of the river. "This is Chicago's first step," wrote a prophetic *Daily News* editorialist, "towards realizing the latent beauties of its river. The group of new buildings being constructed along Wacker Drive is in striking contrast to the north bank, where switch yards and smoke-stained buildings skirt the water's edge, but where handsome structures someday will stand." (FEA)

THE SOUTH BANK of the Chicago River, South Water Street, had for years been the city's food distribution market. As far back as 1909, Daniel Burnham's *Plan of Chicago* had proposed replacing it with a broad boulevard, double-decked and sweeping toward Michigan Avenue. There were lawsuits and disputes but, with chairman of the Chicago Plan Commission Charles H. Wacker as prime mover, the huge project got under way in 1924. August 24, 1925, was the market's final day before being moved elsewhere. (KC)

REVIVED AMONGST THE TALK and actualities of all the physical changes was the oft-discussed idea of building a Chicago subway. Shortly after he was inaugurated mayor on April 16, 1923, William E. Dever (center) went with various city officials into the city's tunnels to pose for photographs and predict that before long work would begin on such a project. It would be two decades more before the city would get its first subway. (CDN)

A LAST LOOK at the old Union Station at Adams and Canal streets before it was demolished for another project proposed in the Chicago Plan: In its stead, in 1924, was built its $65-million successor, with train sheds and tracks covering six square blocks and through which an estimated 66,000 passengers would pass every day. So impressive was the new station, still standing today, that it was unnecessary, stated the *Chicagoan,* to install the customary spittons or "No Spitting" signs because "spitters are impressed by the sheer elegance of their environment." (KC)

STATE STREET, as ever, continued to be the heart of the shopping district (although in time smart shops and boutiques would spring up on the new Michigan Avenue). Yet, the building surge of the 1920s also affected this street, especially its Palmer House, on the left, that had gone up after the Great Fire to become one of the most renowned hotels in the world. This is a view shortly before it was torn down in 1925 to make room for a much sleeker, modern establishment. (KC)

VEHICLES OF THE TIMES: In 1922, the Peoples Gas Light and Coke Company began a home-economics department and, to publicize it, sent this truck equipped with a kitchen to all parts of the city to give curbside cooking demonstrations and to advertise its indoor cooking program at neighborhood stores. For most of the 1920s the *Daily News* maintained a sanitarium in Lincoln Park to which it transported ailing and slum youngsters for treatment, entertainment, and healthy lunches. One of the pleasures of the era was to ride atop a Chicago Motor Coach Company bus on a sunny Chicago day, as these citizens are doing with only one or two giving a glance to that foremost of civic monuments, the Water Tower. (PGC-FEA-CTA)

TWO GRANT PARK PROJECTS of the 1920s, framed here by the Michigan Avenue skyline, were Soldier Field and the Field Museum of Natural History. The museum, originally started with a $1-million gift from Marshall Field in the onetime Palace of Fine Arts after the end of the World's Columbian Exposition, got a new home in 1921 and has remained one of the finest of its kind, with a vast and ever-growing collection of exhibits on zoology, anthropology, botany, and geology. Its building was designed by Daniel H. Burnham. Soldier Field, to the south, was built from 1922 to 1925 and officially christened by former Illinois governor Frank O. Lowden in honor of Chicago's fallen soldiers. Capable of holding 110,000, it has been the scene of innumerable events, the most varied of the 1920s being the 28th Eucharistic Congress in 1926 and the second heavyweight championship fight between Jack Dempsey and Gene Tunney in 1927. (FEA)

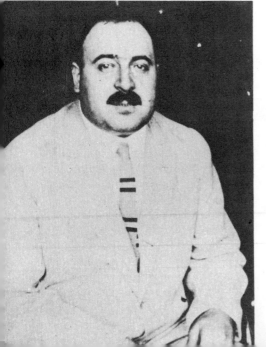

NO LOOK BACKWARD can be complete or authentic without recalling the prolonged gangland wars of Chicago's 1920s. They can be said to have started with the slaying on May 11, 1920, of the city's prime gang chieftain, "Big Jim" Colosimo, in the office behind his well-patronized South Wabash Avenue cafe. Lore—and police authorities—have it that the killer was a young hoodlum whom Colosimo's righthand man Johnny Torrio had imported from Brooklyn and was known as Al Brown, but whose actual name was Al Capone. With Colosimo dead, Torrio tightened control over the huge brothel-booze-and-gambling empire he had helped build and established what came to be known as the Syndicate. Throughout the decade, the carnage and rival-gang wars, the corruption of police and politicians, and the expansion of the murderous and evil role of Capone added to the city's image as one of the wickedest in the world. (KC)

AMID THE MURDERS of such gang bosses as Dion O'Banion, head of the North Side combine; the three Genna brothers, Angelo, Tony, and Mike; mean-tempered Hymie Weiss and dozens of others; and attempts on the life of Johnny Torrio—amid all this, one that aroused civic indignation was that of William J. McSwiggin, an assistant state's attorney with a reputation as a crime-fighter. McSwiggin, nevertheless, was known to be close to members of the Klondike O'Donnell gang, and on the night of April 27, 1926, he and two O'Donnell cohorts met a burst of machine-gun fire outside the Pony Inn in Cicero. This was the first gangland murder in which a machine gun was used, and Capone himself wielded the weapon. He disappeared for four months, and when he returned the police could find no evidence linking him with the crime. (KC)

THE LAST TO DEFY CAPONE was George "Bugs" Moran, successor to O'Banion and Weiss as leader of the North Side band of thieves, hijackers, and bootleggers. On the morning of St. Valentine's Day 1929, killers, two of them dressed as police-men, strode into a North Clark Street garage, and machine-gunned to death six of Moran's henchmen—the Gusenberg brothers, Frank and Pete, Jim Clark, John May, Adam Hyer, and Alfred Weinshank—and a young optometrist, Dr. Reinhart Schwimmer, an old friend of Moran's and a "gangster fan." "Only Capone kills like that," blurted Moran, who had missed being in the garage by minutes. Capone had a perfect alibi: He was then in Miami talking to the local district attorney. But crime experts have always been certain that he was the mastermind and that the killers were led by his ace assassins, John Scalisi and Albert Anselmi. (RF)

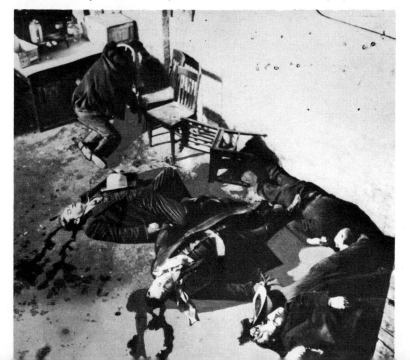

[127]

ANOTHER CRIMINAL receiving worldwide attention in the 1920s was Thomas "Terrible Tommy" O'Connor. Late in September 1921, this cruel and crafty thief was sentenced to the gallows for the murder of Detective Sgt. Patrick J. O'Neill. The following December 11, only four days before he was to be hanged, he and three other prisoners overpowered six guards in this old Cook County Jail and escaped. And he has never been found, despite hundreds of reports in all parts of the country over the years that he had been sighted. (FEA)

CLARENCE DARROW, for years the city's foremost practitioner of criminal law, pleaded many cases but all of them paled alongside one he undertook in 1924 called the "Crime of the Century." In it, two brilliant University of Chicago students, Nathan Leopold and Richard Loeb, kidnapped and murdered thirteen-year-old Bobby Franks, who lived near them in the exclusive Hyde Park area. They confessed after two *Daily News* reporters, James Mulroy and Alvin Goldstein, discovered that a ransom note had been typed on Leopold's typewriter. In a dramatic trial, State's Attorney Robert E. Crowe demanded death for the accused killers. Darrow, seen here with Leopold (left) and Loeb, in a rare photograph by the *Tribune's* Russell V. Hamm, pleaded them guilty, offering thennovel evidence and testimony based on psychiatric data and examinations. The two were sentenced to life terms. Loeb was slashed to death in 1936 in a Joliet penitentiary razor fight. Leopold, after a highly creditable record in prison, was paroled early in 1938 and spent the rest of his life until 1971 working and writing in Puerto Rico. (CPPA)

ANOTHER IMPORTANT CASE of the skillful Darrow was one in 1922 growing out of the scandalous mayoral regime of "Big Bill" Thompson. Darrow (right) defended Fred "Poor Swede" Lundin, Thompson's closest advisor, on charges of fraud in connection with the misappropriation of hundreds of thousands of dollars in school funds. Lundin won acquittal, as did many of Darrow's clients. (CHS)

SPORTS HEROES were plentiful in the twenties. One was Harold "Red" Grange, seen here at far left on the memorable afternoon of October 18, 1924, as he headed for the goal line in one of five touchdown runs he made for the University of Illinois as the Illini overwhelmed the University of Michigan. After the "Galloping Ghost" became a member of the Chicago Bears in 1925, he starred in many games at Soldier Field. Grange was a millionaire three years after he turned professional. Another was a local boy, Johnny Weissmuller, ace of the Illinois Athletic Club's swimming team, who broke record after record and went on to the Olympics and international fame. Between 1921 and 1929 when, at twenty-four, he quit competitive swimming, Weissmuller shattered sixty-seven world records. Later, he became the most famous of all the movie Tarzans. (AP)

THE "LONG COUNT" FIGHT, a famous boxing match between Jack Dempsey and Gene Tunney, took place in Soldier Field on September 22, 1927, and still remains one very likely to arouse an argument among fans. In the seventh round, Dempsey, trying hard to regain the title he had lost to Tunney the year before in Philadelphia, landed a left hook that sent the ex-Marine sprawling into a corner. Dempsey, shown here, stood over his foe with referee Dave Barry refusing for five seconds to begin the count until Dempsey went to a neutral corner. Dempsey moved away and Tunney stayed down until the count of nine, and then got up and went on to outpoint Dempsey. (FEA)

"MURDERERS' ROW" of the Chicago Cubs in 1929 consisted of Hazen "Kiki" Cuyler (left), Rogers Hornsby, Riggs Stephenson, and Lewis "Hack" Wilson. Cuyler, Stephenson, and the stubby Wilson were slugging outfielders, Hornsby the second baseman. Under manager Joe McCarthy, the Cubs won the National League pennant that year, but lost in the World Series to the Philadelphia Athletics, led by the wily Connie Mack. (CDN)

THE FABLED literary renaissance that had started thirty years earlier in Chicago was flickering in the early 1920s, and nothing typified this more than the departure of the talented, irrepressible Ben Hecht for New York. Hecht had begun his career on the *Journal;* later he became a foreign correspondent in postwar Berlin and a daily columnist ("1001 Afternoons in Chicago") for the *Daily News.* He had written playlets, short stories, and novels, notably *Erik Dorn,* and from mid-1923 until June 1924, when he left, he and his sometime-friend, the poet Maxwell Bodenheim, published the ribald, saucy *Chicago Literary Times.* This departure party for Hecht—he is standing fifth from the left with a cigar—was held at Schlogl's restaurant on Wells Street, and among the guests are *Daily News* managing editor Henry Justin Smith (against the rear mirror), Keith Preston, John Gunther, Charles Collins, historian Lloyd Lewis (at far right), lawyer-poet Philip R. Davis, Dr. Morris Fishbein, and drama critic Ashton Stevens, who wrote in the *American* that Chicago ought to fly its flags at half-mast because Hecht was leaving town. (MF)

ONE OF THE FIGURES in the Chicago Literary Renaissance who did not leave town was Harriet Monroe, seen in 1929 at her desk in the offices of *Poetry,* the magazine she had founded in 1912. She had paid only fifty cents a line that year, but among the poets who contributed were Vachel Lindsay ("General William Booth Enters Into Heaven"), William Butler Yeats, Rabindranath Tagore, and Ezra Pound. Carl Sandburg's "Chicago Poems," his first ever published, appeared in March 1914, and T. S. Eliot made it in 1915 with "The Love Song of Alfred J. Prufrock," and Edna St. Vincent Millay in 1917 with "Three Lyrics." By the time Miss Monroe died in 1938, her magazine had become world-famous, and its contributors had included such world-renowned writers as Robert Frost, Sara Teasdale, James Joyce, Robinson Jeffers, Archibald MacLeish, D. H. Lawrence, Edgar Lee Masters, and Amy Lowell. (KC)

AMONG NOTED VISITORS was the Prince of Wales during a nationwide tour in October 1924. He was feted at innumerable parties on the Gold Coast and in the rich northern suburbs, and visited with chewing-gum magnate William Wrigley and Mayor Dever, among many, but one of his most pleasurable days, as he later told reporters, was spent in a tour on horseback of the Union Stock Yards with its president Louis F. Swift (right) and Wellington Leavitt, dean of the cattle buyers who had been affiliated since 1875 with the packing company founded by Swift's father, Gustavus F. Swift. (FEA)

MAYOR MEETS MAYOR: Chicago's "Big Bill" Thompson (right), clad in the heavy fur coat he always wore in winter and clutching his characteristic cowboy hat, exchanges words with dapper James T. Walker, New York's chief executive, between halves of the Notre Dame-University of Southern California football game on a chilly November 1929 Saturday in Soldier Field. Thompson was less than two years away from defeat in an effort to win his fourth term; Walker was three years away from resignation forced on him by scandals and corruption uncovered in the Seabury investigations. (KC)

ANOTHER KIND OF VISITOR was this slim young aviator named Charles Augustus Lindbergh. He left college in 1922 at the age of twenty to become an airplane pilot, and in 1925-26 he flew the first air mail route for the post office department's new service from St. Louis to Chicago. He is shown here on arrival at the new Municipal Airport when he and his fellow airmail pilots were flying without instruments and some died when their planes iced up and crashed. Most who survived were saved by their parachutes, and by the time this picture was taken Lindbergh admitted to having bailed out at least four times. Such zeal and fortitude obviously stood Lindbergh in good stead on May 20, 1927, when he took off in the *Spirit of St. Louis,* a monoplane built especially for him, from New York's Roosevelt Field, landing at Paris' Le Bourget Air Field 33 hours, 39 minutes later in the first successful solo flight across the Atlantic Ocean. Amid much international adulation and hoopla, that August he was presented by Mayor Thompson to a crowd of 75,000 that had gathered in Comiskey Park, home of the White Sox baseball team. (CPPA-CDN)

COMMERCIAL AVIATION was still in its infancy but Chicago was prepared. This is Municipal Airport in 1928, a year after it was converted from a cow pasture in the southwest of the city and served as a landing area for Lindbergh and such other pioneers as Wiley Post. Tiny at first, the airfield was expanded several times in ensuing years as travel by air increased. One of the major problems was to relocate railroad tracks that bisected the airport, but this was done by the time the name was changed in 1949 to Midway. (WKC)

THIS PLANE, a Boeing 80-A shown in 1929, was typical of those used in airmail flights by the fledgling United Air Lines. It is shown as it soars above Lake Michigan with the city's skyline framing the background. (UA)

A FLYING MACHINE of a different sort intrigued Chicagoans on August 18, 1929, when the *Graf Zeppelin* visited on its globe-girdling tour. It was estimated that over one million citizens gathered in streets, parks, and on rooftops to watch, wave, and cheer the big German dirigible. The *Daily News'* George Peebles was in Grant Park that day to record this crowd gathered near Buckingham Fountain as the *Graf Zeppelin* soared over the city. (GP)

IN ITS INFANCY, too, was radio. The first artist ever heard on a Chicago broadcast was Mary Garden, the tempestuous operatic diva ("Sarah Bernhardt of the operatic stage," one critic called her). A month after KYW began operations in the Belmont Hotel, she sang and talked from its studios on November 21, 1921. At the piano was Isaac van Grove, and the announcer standing by while Miss Garden, enthralled with the wonder of it all, speaks over the microphone was none other than Milton J. Cross, for decades to come the "Voice of the Metropolitan Opera" on Saturday afternoon broadcasts. (KC)

THE HOTTEST TEAM in Chicago radio, and soon all over the land, was Freeman Gosden (left) and Charles Correll, whose first program was as imitation blacks "Sam 'n' Henry" on the *Tribune's* station WGN in 1928. When they shifted to WMAQ the next year and became "Amos 'n' Andy," they scored an even greater hit, and when the National Broadcasting Company put them on five nights a week—Gosden was the gentle Amos with his plaintive "Awaa, awaaa" and Correll was the pompous Andy with his "Sho' 'nuf" and the Wily Kingfish and Mystic Knights of the Sea—they captivated millions. Movie houses switched off their films so that patrons would not miss a single episode, and some restaurants stopped service during the broadcast. The show's popularity persisted for many years; a decade after it first went on the air, it was estimated to have a nightly audience of over thirty million. (FEA)

A MAJOR CULTURAL VENTURE: Samuel Insull, the city's prime utilities magnate and current civic-social leader, combined his Civic Opera House with offices so that rent from them would support the cost of productions. On Wacker Drive and Madison Street, his edifice (left) in the shape of a huge throne opened on November 4, 1929, with Rosa Raisa starring in *Aida.* That opening night presaged a glorious era of locally produced operas, but the deepening economic depression, the collapse of Insull's empire, and other woes caused a breakup of the opera company and ultimate sale of the $20-million building to an insurance firm. The automobiles and trucks here at the right are lined up outside the Hearst Building where the morning *Herald-Examiner* and the *Evening American* were published. Both are long gone, as is the ugly elevated railroad spur splitting Wacker Drive. (CTA)

[137]

ON A SMALLER SCALE than productions of the Civic Opera Company were those of the avant-garde Chicago Allied Arts, founded in 1924. It was a ballet company of twenty-five—here shown in a 1926 performance at the Eighth Street Theater in honor of the visit of Queen Marie of Roumania—directed by Adolph Bohm, once a dancer with Diaghilev's Ballet Russe troupe, and accompanied by Eric DeLamarter's Orchestra. Concerts preceding ballet performances featured the complex works of such composers as Honegger, Milhaud, Stravinsky, and Schoenberg. Ruth Page was its premier dancer during the unique company's relatively brief life. (FEA)

ALONG THE GOLD COAST and elsewhere, there was much gossip about the McCormicks, Harold and Edith. Mrs. McCormick *(left),* the imperious, eccentric daughter of John D. Rockefeller, presided over Chicago society from her mansion at 1000 Lake Drive, and was given to wearing expensively garish costumes at festive parties. She was once reported to have paid $1 million for a diamond dog collar and matching tiara, and twice as much for a pearl necklace. She and her husband, heir to the McCormick reaper fortune, became increasingly estranged after he fell in love with Ganna Walska, a sexy, strong-willed, but mediocre opera singer. When Mrs. McCormick granted him a divorce in 1921, McCormick took time out for an operation that reportedly would give him the vigorous glands of a younger man for at least fifteen more years. Despite this, his marriage to Ganna was only fairly successful, according to her account some years later. They made many trips together—in 1929 they were heading for Europe *(below)* on the liner *Paris*— but they divorced in 1931, at a cost of $6 million to him. He became, among other things, an expert whistler, good enough to perform on radio and in concert halls, and also, until her death in 1932, sent Edith McCormick a single rose on her every birthday. (FEA)

THE UNIVERSITY OF CHICAGO got a new leader, its youngest and most intellectually adventurous, when Robert Maynard Hutchins, only thirty, became president on November 19, 1929. An innovator, he instituted the New Plan, a four-year liberal arts program giving a full grounding in biological, physical, and social sciences and the humanities the first two years, to be followed by specialized work later. He also introduced the Great Books program, reorganized the graduate school, and abolished football. Inspiring, articulate, and controversial, he served until 1951, his last six years as chancellor, and then left for other assignments, among them the presidency of the Fund for the Republic, the founding of the Center for the Study of Democratic Institutions, the chairmanship of the board of editors of the *Encyclopedia Britannica* and the *Great Books of the Western World.* (UC)

WHEN THE MUSEUM of Science and Industry was begun in 1930, the neglected old Palace of Fine Arts, sole structure remaining of the World's Columbian Exposition of 1893, was assured a new life. A multi-million dollar offer by Julius Rosenwald, head of Sears Roebuck and Company and an ardent philanthropist, had been made to reshape it to what he hoped would be "the greatest technical and industrial museum in the world." Completed in 1933, it continues to be Chicago's number-one tourist attraction year after year, with hundreds of exhibits valued at over $50 million in all, and with fascinating, instructive machines and do-it-yourself contrivances that constitute a vivid array of scientific and industrial triumphs. (GP)

TOWERING SYMBOLS of growth are in this panoramic view looking east along the Chicago River toward Lake Michigan in 1931. Construction since 1921 included (at far left) the Medinah Athletic Club, later the Sheraton-Chicago Hotel; the Tribune Tower; the Wrigley Building; the London Guarantee Building, now the Stone Container Corporation Building; the 333 North Michigan Avenue Building; the Bell Building, now the 75 East Wacker Drive Building; and the Pure Oil Building. (IH)

DESPITE MATERIAL PROGRESS, the city was struck hard by the Great Depression of the 1930s. The dismal years brought about ramshackle clusters of hovels called "Hoovervilles" and street-corner apple merchants and the strangest kind of impromptu shelters for the homeless and jobless, exemplified by these men outside an abandoned limeworks near the Hawthorne racetrack. Of the "Hoovervilles" Edmund Wilson later wrote: "Most were knocked together of tar-paper and tin, old car bodies, old packing boxes, with old stovepipes leaning askew, amid the blackened weeds in the snow and the bones of old rubbish piles. . . . The inhabitants of these wretched settlements chiefly foraged from the city dumps."
(CPPA-KC-CDN)

[141]

ANOTHER ASPECT of the Depression, this kind of scene was not unusual in various parts of the city. In this period, as for decades earlier and later, there was always the Maxwell Street Market, centered at Halsted and Maxwell streets in a confusion of stalls, boxes, wagons, and pushcarts with hundreds upon hundreds of items for sale, from used umbrellas, underwear, and vegetables to bread, frankfurters, shoes, purses, and magazines and books—and at prices that could be lowered through spirited haggling. (JA-KC)

DEPRESSION OR NO, there were innumerable diversions for Chicagoans in those 1930s. One of the "escape" crazes was the dance marathon: an example is this brother-and-sister team's 3,327th hour of an incredible feat that began on August 29, 1930, and continued, with time out for snatches of sleep, into the following April before outlasting all other competitors' efforts. (CDN)

A TIME OF RECKONING came for Al Capone the summer of 1931. A year earlier, he had had himself picked up in Philadelphia for carrying a gun—rumor was that he wanted to escape retribution for the St. Valentine's Day Massacre—and served ten easy months, emerging to find himself labeled U.S. Public Enemy Number One. He tried to settle down in Havana, the Black Hills of South Dakota, and Los Angeles, but in each place he was invited to leave. Returning to Chicago, he was indicted for evading $215,000 in income taxes. Cocky and confident that he could beat the rap, he willingly posed for photographers during a lull in the trial, but he was sentenced to ten years in the penitentiary. Chicago's final glimpse of him was as he began his trip to Atlanta in custody of U.S. Marshal Henry C. W. Laubenheimer. He was later transferred to Alcatraz Prison in San Francisco Bay, and then released after serving eight years. (RF-CPPA)

[143]

HOLLYWOOD VISITORS early in the 1930s included the rarely-photographed Greta Garbo, seen here after she acceded to a request by *Herald-Examiner* photographer Jimmy Quinn to open the door of her Pullman stateroom in the Union Station just long enough for him to take a quick shot. When she did so, six other photographers got their pictures but Quinn was not quick enough. (EM)

TWO OTHER MOVIE STARS: Mae West *(below)* went down into the Chicago Freight Tunnel for a ride with an assortment of city officials and celebrity hounds in the same era that Jean Harlow *(right)* languidly posed here on the deck of the *Mizpah,* a luxury yacht owned by Chicago industrialist Eugene McDonald. (KC-RF)

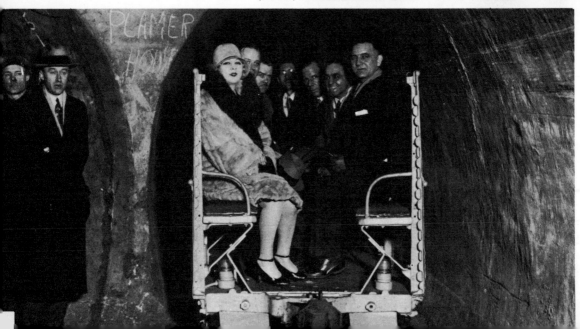

TO LINCOLN PARK in 1931 came Bushman, an African gorilla who would be the park zoo's outstanding attraction for more than two decades. Shortly after his arrival, Bushman, then two years old and weighing sixty pounds, was installed behind a camera while the zoo director Alfred E. Parker sat for a portrait and *Tribune* photographer Edward McGill recorded it all. Jumping forward some twenty years, the full-grown Bushman was photographed memorably by the *Sun-Times'* David Mann, as he munched nonchalantly on a stalk of celery. Bushman by then weighed 575 pounds and stood 6 feet, 2 inches tall, and his value was placed between $100,000 and $250,000. On January 1, 1951, after battling arthritis, heart disease, and old age, Bushman died in his sleep; taxidermists reconstructed him and he is on permanent display in the Field Museum of Natural History. (EM-FEA)

OAFISH "BIG BILL" Thompson was deep in a bitter mayoral contest with his Democratic challenger, shrewd Anton J. "Tony" Cermak, when he staged a miniature rodeo in the City Council chambers on February 2, 1931, before Cermak whipped him and sent him into political oblivion. (WKC)

[146]

THE CLIMACTIC CLOSING of the Democratic presidential convention on June 30, 1932, in the Chicago Stadium: New York's governor, Franklin D. Roosevelt, is making his acceptance speech, which he had written on a storm-tossed, nine-hour flight from Albany. Vowing to take "unprecedented actions" to cure the Depression, and expressing hope that his party would seek to break "absurd traditions," he intoned in that unforgettable voice: "I pledge you, I pledge myself, to a New Deal for the American people!" That October, a month before Roosevelt defeated incumbent Pres. Herbert Hoover, statistics revealed that Chicago was one of the hardest-hit cities in the prevailing depression, with 750,000 unemployed, the weekly cost of state relief at $1.5 million, and only 51 of the city's 228 banks still open. (EM)

ON THE CAMPAIGN TRAIL, Roosevelt managed to take in the third game of the World Series between the Chicago Cubs and the New York Yankees, a memorable contest because it was the one in which Babe Ruth pointed with his bat to the specific spot in Wrigley Field where he intended to land a home run— and did! The Democratic presidential candidate and Mrs. Roosevelt were the guests of Mayor Anton J. Cermak and posed smilingly before the game with the Cubs' manager, Charlie Grimm (left), and Joe McCarthy, manager of the winning Yankees. (CPPA)

MAYOR CERMAK exults in Roosevelt's victory on the night of election that November 1932. Cermak would be the victim of an assassin's bullet aimed the following February 15 at President-elect Roosevelt in Miami. His funeral was one of the longest and most spectacular in Chicago's history. On orders of Patrick J. Nash, powerful chairman of the Cook County Democratic central committee, the City Council appointed Edward J. "Big Ed" Kelly, president of the South Park Board, to fill out Cermak's term. Kelly won his first full term in 1935, defeating Emil C. Wetten by an astounding 622,000 votes out of 862,000, and then ruled in City Hall for another twelve years. (RF)

GOV. HENRY HORNER (right), elected in 1932 in the Roosevelt landslide, with "Big Ed" Kelly (left) and Patrick J. Nash at a political dinner during a time of party peace: In 1936, these two Democratic bosses sought to keep Horner from running for a second term, reportedly because the governor had vetoed a bill to license racing handbooks. Horner refused to yield and ran anyway, denouncing Kelly and Nash as "penthouse pirates and corruptionists." After a spirited campaign, Horner defeated the party's official candidate Dr. Herman N. Bundesen by 160,000 votes and compelled Kelly and Nash to support him in his successful bid for relection. (KC)

DEFYING THE DEPRESSION, Chicago opened its A Century of Progress exposition on May 27, 1933, after nearly a decade of on-and-off planning. On some 400 man-made acres along Lake Michigan, extending three miles south of Soldier Field, stood exhibits, scientific buildings, attractions that ranged from a diamond mine to a golden-roofed Lamaist temple from Jehol, an inevitable Midway, and innumerable examples of severe modern architecture. On opening day, a detachment from the Great Lakes U. S. Naval Training Station paraded down the Avenue of Flags, and the fair's president, Rufus C. Dawes, hailed the exposition as "the spontaneous expression of the pride of the citizenship of Chicago." (RF)

Problems and Progress: 1933 to 1955

"RAINBOW CITY flaunts to the sky the boldest hues of the spectrum, in audacious and sometimes cock-eyed forms. Bathed in extraordinary effects of light, they signal Chicago's invincible optimism. . . ."

Thus said the *Literary Digest,* in reporting on the Century of Progress exposition that the city staged on the Lake Michigan shore in 1933-34, in the midst of the Great Depression. Planning had started in 1929, and no financial debacle nor hordes of unemployed could daunt its backers. The intent was to show man's advancements in science, communication, transportation, and the arts during the century since Chicago had been incorporated as a village. "Within this hundred years," intoned the fair's president, Rufus C. Dawes, "all the conditions of human living have been altered. And now that this city, the product of these influences, has reached its centenary, these victories deserve a triumphant celebration."

A celebration it surely was, with an influx of thirty-eight million visitors. Amazingly, under the direction of a highly-organized ex-army major, Lenox Lohr, the exposition not only thrived, but was the only one of its kind in the history of civic extravaganzas to return a profit to its investors.

But the Depression persisted, curtailing plans for civic improvements and public works and, as in the years after the World's Columbian Exposition of 1893, creating tensions between working men and industrialists that erupted into a violence that was signalized by the fatal shooting of ten men outside the Republic Steel plant's gates on Memorial Day 1937.

There were some brighter aspects. Late in the 1930s, federal funds enabled construction of huge, public housing projects designed to take low-income families out of decrepit slum homes. The $7-million Jane Addams Homes went up in 1938, and then, at the start 1941, the biggest yet, the Ida B. Wells Homes on forty acres, and, in 1942, the Frances Cabrini Homes. A revitalized Chicago Plan Commission made proposals for improvements

including a subway system to alleviate growing transportation problems, and the first leg of that system was begun, to be completed in 1943.

With the onset of war in Europe, Chicago was a kind of citadel for opponents to America's participation in any way. But after the attack on Pearl Harbor, debate and dissension became academic, and the city furnished many hundreds of thousands for the armed services. It was the country's most hospitable center for those in transit to training camps and eventually Europe or the Pacific, and it sold more war bonds and gathered more salvage materials than any other city.

The war brought sudden prosperity, as in earlier generations, with Chicago's location as the hub of transportation and of massive output of war materials again proving vital. A glimmer of future problems was evident when some industries set up their plants in areas outside the city limits. Early in the war, a momentous event occurred at the University of Chicago where, beneath a Stagg Field grandstand, a year's experimentation by scientists was climaxed in the first successful test of the control of atomic power.

Postwar prosperity prevailed, and so did problems. There were racial tensions, police scandals, and insufficient housing, the latter despite the inauguration of slum clearance and urban renewal ventures. So more low-income housing was provided—to be denounced later by experts as "slums in the sky"—and private investors took initial steps in the early 1950s to create racially integrated, middle-class developments such as Lake Meadows and Prairie Shores on the near south side. The subway system was expanded; a multi-million-dollar school construction program was instituted; and plans were drawn to make the city one of the world's major medical centers. In its eternal role in transportation, Chicago accommodated the burgeoning air traffic by making provisions for a new, larger field to supplement—eventually to supplant—Midway Airport, and it began to broaden its port facilities.

Critics were omnipresent as always, typified by *New Yorker* magazine's A. J. Liebling, who spent an unhappy year and wrote testily of Chicago as "The Second City." Reactions ranged from anger, to indifference, to scorn, to counter-ridicule, and no one was more determined to dispel that notion than a tough-minded, chauvinistic politician who had slowly climbed in the strong Cook County Democratic organization to where he had become its boss and, in 1955, the city's mayor. His name was Richard Joseph Daley, and from then on Chicago would never, never again be the same.

Facing page: THE FAIR'S ATTRACTION that soon had the whole town and much of the nation talking was Sally Rand. Shortly before the exposition, she had appeared as Lady Godiva at an art students' ball, and received a lot of publicity after being barred from prancing into the ball on her horse named Mike. So she conceived the notion of doing a dance with nothing to hide her nudity but a couple of ostrich-feather fans. From the start she was a sensation at the Streets of Paris, drawing nearly 75,000 customers the first month and boosting her weekly wages from $175 to $3,000 by summer's end. "A lot of boobs come to see a woman wiggle with a fan or without fig leaves," said a judge in denying an injunction to stop her, "but we have these boobs and we have a right to cater to them." Sally was proud of her figure and posed for friendly photographers like the *Herald-Examiner's* Ralph Frost. She continued as a star in fan and bubble dancing for years saying, "I haven't been without work a day since I took off my pants." (RF)

A MAJOR FEATURE of the Century of Progress exposition was the Sky Ride *(left)*. Its twin towers rose sixty-four stories—"highest man-made structure west of Manhattan," boasted the fair's publicitors—and each day many thousands lined up to ride the "rocker cars" across the expanse of the fair grounds. The Sky Ride was the fair's parallel to the famous Ferris wheel at the World's Columbian Exposition of 1893, and from it could be seen not only all of the exposition but the city to the north, notably the Field Museum of Natural History, the Grant Park bandshell—so new that it was still without benches—and, beyond, the Buckingham Fountain and the famous skyline along Michigan Avenue. (KC-GP)

AMONG MANY foreign visitors was one of Mussolini's flying aces, Gen. Italo Balbo, who led a contingent of twenty-four seaplanes to the exposition and for whom fair officials staged a big dinner at the Stevens Hotel (later the Conrad Hilton). Balbo is the bearded, bemedaled fellow talking with an interpreter and flanked by Mr. and Mrs. Rufus C. Dawes. Although anti-Fascist organizations protested, Balbo made an impression so strong that Seventh Street, alongside the hotel, was renamed Balbo Drive. (RF)

[154]

SO SUCCESSFUL was A Century of Progress that Dawes and his managers decided to keep it open another year, and 1934 too defied pessimistic predictions. When the fair closed and the job of dismantling it began with the dynamiting of the Sky Ride's east tower as seen in Harry Coleman's vivid photograph, it had drawn nearly forty million visitors and returned a profit to its backers—the only fair of its kind ever to do so. (RF)

ONE OF THE WORST FIRES since the Great Fire of 1871 occurred on May 19, 1934, when flames devastated the eastern section of the Union Stock Yards and adjoining territory, and threatened for a time to engulf much of the crowded surrounding South Side. Over three square miles were covered by the flames. Thousands of head of cattle and other animals were destroyed and scores of firemen were overcome by heat. Total damage came to more than eight million dollars. (FEA)

TWO FAMOUS FIGHTS in the 1930s: Here, on June 23, 1933, Barney Ross, a perennial Chicago favorite who made his way up from the West Side ghetto, has his arm raised in victory by announcer Al Smith after defeating Tony Canzoneri for the lightweight championship. Ross' longtime friend and co-manager, Art Winch, stands nearby. Four years later, and almost to the very night, Joe Louis is waved to his corner in the eighth round of his winning battle in Comiskey Park against heavyweight champion James J. Braddock. "In that eighth," Braddock said later, "I had nothing left. When he hit me with that right, I just lay there, I couldn't have got up if they'd offered me a million dollars." (FEA-CPPA)

THE CHICAGO BLACK HAWKS had to wait eight years after they played their first National Hockey League game in 1926 at the Coliseum, but on April 10, 1934, they won their first Stanley Cup, defeating Detroit, 1 to 0, before a crowd of 16,500 that saw Mush March score the game's only goal in overtime. One of the stellar members of the 1934 team was Charles "Chuck" Gardiner, then considered the best goalkeeper in the business. (RF)

BASEBALL HEROES were headed in the late 1930s by this star battery of the Chicago Cubs—Jerome "Dizzy" Dean (right), the man with the blazing fastball, and Leo "Gabby" Hartnett, the efficient and highly popular man behind the plate. For $185,000 and three players, Dean had come to the Cubs in 1938 after several fantastically successful years with the St. Louis Cardinals and, that year, he and Hartnett were instrumental in helping the Cubs win another National League pennant. (RF)

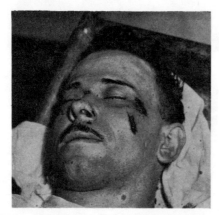

THE GREAT CHASE for John Dillinger, the desperado who had terrorized the Midwest, ended on the hot night of July 22, 1934, when he was shot to death by federal agents and Chicago police minutes after emerging from the Biograph Theater, where he had enjoyed Clark Gable in *Manhattan Melodrama,* with Anna Sage —the "Lady in Red" alleged to have fingered Dillinger for the waiting lawmen. Hundreds of the curious were permitted by Coroner Frank J. Walsh to view Dillinger's bullet-riddled corpse as it lay in the Cook County Morgue. (WS)

VIOLENT DEATH came, too, to Vincent Gebardi, better known as "Machine Gun" Jack McGurn, who served Al Capone loyally as chief of his death squad. After Capone's downfall and penitentiary sentence, McGurn continued to operate in and out of the rackets. Obviously he must have angered someone, for on a February night in 1936, while quietly awaiting his turn in a Milwaukee Avenue bowling alley, he was fatally shot in the back of his head. (WKC)

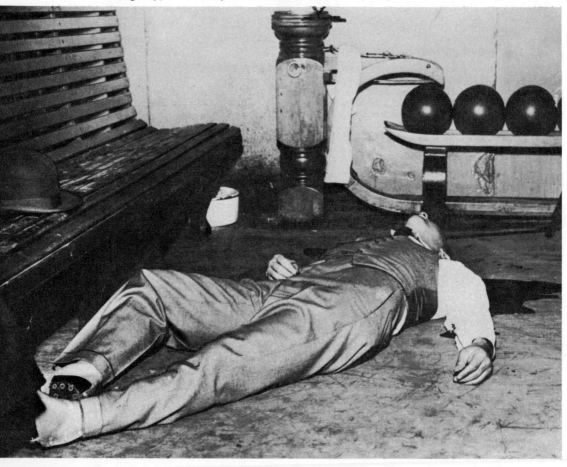

ONE MURDER MYSTERY in Chicago involved this noted physician, Dr. Alice Lindsay Wynekoop. On the murky night of November 20, 1933, she summoned an undertaker, saying that her daughter-in-law Rheta had suddenly died. When investigation showed Rheta had been shot to death, Dr. Wynekoop claimed thieves must have killed her in a search for her supply of narcotics. But this story and others of the doctor proved false and, in a sensation-packed trial, prosecutors convinced a jury that Dr. Wynekoop committed the murder because she wanted to free her son Earle to marry another woman. She was sentenced to twenty-five years. Paroled in 1946, she avowed that she would clear herself and name "the real murderer," but by the time she died on July 4, 1955, under an assumed name in a nursing home, she had been more or less forgotten except by those who still wondered, "Did Dr. Alice really do it?" (WKC)

A SAD DAY for a once-mighty Chicagoan: In the wake of the Great Depression, Samuel Insull's several stock-holding companies collapsed and thousands of investors, who had revered him, lost all they had. Investigations began, but Insull was already in Europe, where he was to be arrested. "I have committed no crime," he said. "The failure of my companies was not fraudulent. I have just been unfortunate and lost lots of money. More than $100 million of it was my own." Returned to Chicago in 1934 and unable to post $250,000 bond on state and federal charges, he was taken to the Cook County Jail, as shown here. He and sixteen associates wen on trial for using the mails to defraud and, after lengthy and complex testimony, he was acquitted. By 1938 when he died, he left debts of $14,000 and assets of less than $1,000. (CPPA)

DESPITE "NEW DEAL" MEASURES that helped curb economic distress, there were still protests and marches in the streets. Typical of those in the mid-1930s was this mass parade of jobless blacks and whites. (KC)

[160] THE BLOODIEST, BITTEREST EVENT of the decade was the Memorial Day Massacre in 1937. John L. Lewis' new labor-union aggregation, the Congress of Industrial Organizations, was in the midst of an organizing drive among steelworkers on the far South Side. About 25,000 were out on strike but, at Republic Steel Corporation, 1,000 non-striking employes still reported daily. On Memorial Day, May 30, a few hundred strikers and sympathizers including women and children, gathered there and started to set up a picket line, some carrying clubs, some rocks, many with American flags and signs. When on a field adjoining the plant they were met by armed policemen, someone threw a rock, someone else shouted curses, and soon there were shots and more shots from the police ranks. Ten men in the crowd were killed, many wounded. Despite a coroner's verdict of "justifiable homicide," a Congressional investigation charged police with instituting the fatal clash and using "excessive force." (KC)

ON HIS WAY to dedicate the Outer Drive Link
Bridge on October 5, 1937, President Roosevelt
rode with Bishop Bernard J. Sheil, one of the city's
revered prelates and founder of the Catholic Youth
Organization. Roosevelt, seeking to marshall more
public opinion against Adolph Hitler's depredations in Europe, made his famous "Quarantine the
aggressor" speech that day, saying: "The epidemic
of world lawlessness is spreading. When an epidemic of physical disease starts to spread, the community approves and joins in a quarantine of
patients in order to protect the health of the
community against the spread of the disease."
Reaction was instant and mostly hostile. A great
many of the letters and telegrams to the White
House accused the President of being a "warmon-
ger." (WS)

DURING HIS STAY for the bridge dedication,
President Roosevelt was the guest of the learned
and forthright Cardinal George Mundelein, head
of the vast Catholic archdiocese for over two
decades. A foe of all bigotry, Cardinal Mundelein
spoke out often through *New World,* the arch-
diocesan weekly, against anti-Semitism, and the
previous May he had derided Adolf Hitler as "an
Austrian paperhanger, and a poor one at that."
Although the German government formally protested to the Vatican and the United States, both
took the stand that private utterances were not
official—and Cardinal Mundelein neither retracted
the statement nor apologized. (FEA)

FROM THE START of Hitler's rise in Germany and throughout Europe, he had many sympathizers and supporters in Chicago and the Middle West. Fritz Kuhn, leader of the German-American Bund (seated second from right), often appeared as chief speaker at rallies complete with Nazi-style trappings. (KC)

IN SPITE OF THE DEPRESSION, labor strife, and gathering war clouds, Chicagoans found considerable pleasure in a variety of entertainers. These fellows that set a pattern for a persisting Chicago-style of humor are the "Three Doctors"—Russell Pratt (left), Ransom Sherman, and Joe Rudolph. They delighted radio listeners with impudent skits, ad-lib humor, and takeoffs on current events and lyrics of popular songs. The team broke up in the mid-1930s, but Sherman was a hit on network television and movies as a performer and writer well into the 1940s. (FEA)

SOAP OPERAS were very big in Chicago in the 1930s,
and continued so for at least two decades more. NBC's
"Guilding Light" originated here, and among those in
the cast of the Monday-through-Friday, heart-tugging
drama series was the future Oscar winner, Mercedes
McCambridge (second from left). Others in the scene
are Arthur Peterson, Helen Behmiller, and Mignon
Schreiber. (FEA)

EXTREMELY POPULAR on local station WENR
and then on the National Broadcasting Company network were Jim and Marian Jordan as "Fibber McGee
and Molly." Here, flanking Bill Thompson, their
dialectitian on the program, they were setting out for
Hollywood in April 1937, to make the first of several
movies, *This Way, Please.* They continued to be a top-
ranking comedy team on radio and then on television
for years. (FEA)

ANOTHER AUDIENCE-PLEASER was Paul
Rhymer's "Vic and Sade," for several years one
of the country's most popular radio serials. In the
daily shows, Rhymer, as Ray Bradbury later
wrote, "dramatized lovingly and forever middle-
class America as it existed in the 1930s." The
cast included Art Van Harvey (left) as Vic,
Clarence L. Hartzell as Uncle Fletcher, Bernadine
Flynn as Sade, and Bill Idelson as Vic and Sade's
son, Rush. (KC)

[163]

MUSICAL ROYALTY of the 1930s: Benny Goodman, who took his first clarinet lessons as a boy in short pants at Hull House, later returned to appear at the Congress Hotel's Pompeian Room and on the stage of the Chicago Theater as the "King of Swing," while Wayne King, shown here as he played for his singer Berenice Parks, had been popular since the late 1920s as the "Waltz King" and continued to draw big crowds to the Gold Coast Room of the august Drake Hotel. (KC-FEA)

THE PRIZE PRODUCTION of the WPA Federal Theater in the late 1930s was an all-black takeoff of *The Mikado.* Labeled *The Swing Mikado,* it imparted syncopation to Sir Arthur Sullivan's music, gave extra meaning to W. S. Gilbert's lyrics, and scored a hit to parallel anything on Broadway. It played for twenty-one soldout weeks in Chicago, then went to New York for a long run. In this scene, Edward Fraction (in top hat) is the Mikado, and directly in front of him are Maurice Cooper as Nanki-Poo and Gladys Boucree as Yum-Yum. (KC)

AS A RAILROAD CENTER, Chicago in the 1930s still remained the nation's first. The total daily average came close to 1,500 inbound and outbound passenger trains. One of the most famous was the Sante Fe Chief, shown arriving on the dot at the Dearborn Street Depot. Two others equally renowned, and engaged in a race on the Chicago-New York route, were the Pennsylvania Railroad's Broadway Limited and the New York Central's Twentieth Century, shown here south of the Englewood station enroute to Manhattan. (RF-PR)

[165]

IN GENTLE CONTRAST to skyscrapers, factories, and businesses were such places as the Italian Court, a slightly rococo cluster of artists' studios, shops, and apartments on North Michigan Avenue. Irene Castle, the dance queen of an earlier generation, lived there until she wed the coffee millionaire Frederic McLaughlin and moved to the North Shore suburbs, and poetess Mrs. William Vaughn Moody, wife of a famous University of Chicago English professor, held poetry readings in her delightful basement restaurant, Le Petit Gourmet. In its forty-five years or more before it was torn down in 1969, the Italian Court was a natural subject for painters and photographers. The *Tribune's* Edward McGill recorded this charming view. (EM)

THE ROOSEVELT STEAMROLLER got going at the 1940 Democratic presidential convention with the help of Thomas Dennis Garry, city superintendent of sewers. On orders of Mayor Kelly, Garry crawled beneath the speakers platform at Chicago Stadium, fashioned a hookup to the loudspeaker system and for twenty minutes bellowed: "Illinois wants Roosevelt! Mayor Kelly wants Roosevelt! Everybody wants Roosevelt!" The deed delighted many, offended some, and helped to galvanize the assemblage into nominating FDR for his third term. (CST)

IN THE 1940 CAMPAIGN few of its many dramatic events matched the disgraceful egg-splattering of Republican candidate Wendell Willkie when he arrived at the La Salle Street Station. Borrie Kanter, then a *Times* photographer, was on hand, and his record of the act was placed on the newspaper's front page with a statement by editor Richard J. Finnegan: "Deepest apologies to you, Mr. Willkie. The whole town is genuinely sorry and ashamed for the action of this single ONE of its three-and-a-half million citizens." (FEA)

AN AERIAL VIEW in 1940 of the central commercial district fronted by the sprawling light-colored Montgomery Ward and Company complex on the north branch of the Chicago River: The buildings on the south of Chicago Avenue (right) housed the general administrative offices and a

large department store; the others were those in which mail orders were assembled and shipped, often at the rate of 200,000 a day. Visible between the Montgomery Ward plant and Lake Michigan in the background is much of the city's business and financial area. (CAC)

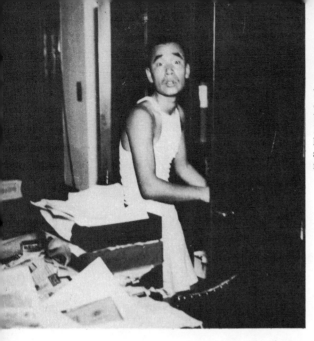

WITHIN AN HOUR after the bombing of Pearl Harbor on December 7, 1941, Japanese consulates everywhere began swiftly to pack papers and belongings. George Kotalik, an enterprising young *Times* photographer, hustled to the office of the Japanese consul, barged in, and caught this staff member by utter surprise as he was rummaging through his locker. (FEA)

ON DECEMBER 2, 1942, at 3:25 p.m., after years of experiments, the brilliant physicist Enrico Fermi and a team of scientists at the University of Chicago achieved the first self-sustaining nuclear chain reaction, through the use of uranium in a graphite pile. For twenty-eight minutes in an abandoned squash court at Stagg Field, they released the energy of the atom's nucleus, controlled that energy — and initiated the Atomic Age. No photographs are known to exist. This is Douglas M. Parrish's painting of Fermi and the others, who included Nobel prizewinner Arthur Holly Compton, Walter H. Zinn, Leo Szilard, Herbert A. Anderson, E. P. Wigner, Norman Hilberry, and George Weil. (IBT)

CHICAGO WAS also a site for shipbuilding activity from the earliest days of World War II. Here, with the city's famous amusement park Riverview close by, a subchaser built in the Grebe shipyards and destined for use by the British is launched in the north branch of the Chicago River. (RF)

AS EVERYWHERE in the nation during World War II, there was intense homefront activity of varied kinds in Chicago. Here, men from the Works Progress Administration load old scrap iron beds into trucks after nearly five tons of them had been collected at the Parkway Community House on the South Side. (FEA)

NEWSPAPER RIVALRY, always intense in Chicago since its earliest days, was heightened with the establishment on December 4, 1941, of the *Chicago Sun* by philanthropist Marshall Field III, here (left) with the paper's publisher Silliman Evans after the first issue rolled off the presses. (KC)

FIELD'S PRIME OPPONENT was Col. Robert Rutherford Mc Cormick and the mighty *Tribune,* first established in 1847 and ever since an important influence in the city. Seen here against the impressive background of Tribune Tower as he made a patriotic speech is Colonel McCormick, who fought Field vigorously, even attempting in vain to keep him from securing an Associated Press franchise. Field persisted, spent many millions to keep the *Sun* alive, and ultimately bought the *Times* in 1948 to create the *Sun-Times,* which has continued successfully as the *Tribune's* competitor. (KC)

AN INTERLUDE during wartime found Frederick Stock conducting a recording session in 1942 with famed pianist Artur Schnabel and members of the Chicago Symphony Orchestra. Stock had been associated with the symphony since 1895, first as a cellist and, after 1905, as its conductor. Equally well-known as a composer and introducer of new musical compositions, Stock died of a heart attack a few weeks after this photograph was taken. (FEA)

CHICAGO GOT A SUBWAY, finally, on October 17, 1942, after years of campaigns and discussion. At the dedication of the $34-million, five-mile underground, Mayor Kelly happily officiated, flanked by Joshua D'Esposito representing the federal funding agency, the Public Works Administration; B. J. Fallon, head of the Chicago Rapid Transit Company that undertook operation of the line; Alderman James Quinn, chairman of the City Council transportation committee; and Philip J. Harrington, city commissioner of subways and superhighways. The second subway, Milwaukee-Dearborn-Congress, went into operation in 1951 at a cost of $40 million. (CTA)

[173]

BITTERLY INVOLVED with the wartime federal government over nonobservance of regulations imposed by the War Labor Board, Sewell Avery, Mongtomery Ward and Company's chairman, refused to heed directives because he maintained that his firm was not doing war work. The plant was consequently seized on the morning of April 27, 1944, but Avery declined to leave. On orders of the Army officer in charge, two GIs were sent to lift the stubborn industrialist out of his chair and carry him outside—a rather remarkable event, recorded by William Pauer of the *Times*. (FEA)

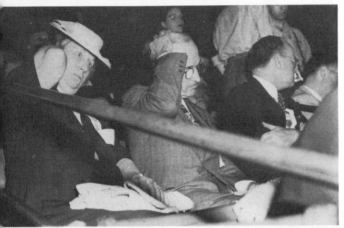

AT THE DEMOCRATIC CONVENTION in 1944, Harry S. Truman (center), then U.S. senator from Missouri, waits word whether President Roosevelt will select him as running-mate in the oncoming race. In this informal shot at the Chicago Stadium, he and his wife Bess are seated near a Missouri friend, John W. Snyder. Word came soon enough, after Missouri's other senator, Bennett Champ Clark, placed Truman's name in nomination and the doughty Truman came to the podium admidst the waving of signs and sustained cheers. (FEA-CST)

ALTHOUGH HE WAS not in good health, President Roosevelt campaigned hard. One of his most enthusiastic receptions was in Soldier Field, where, after exchanging these greetings with Mayor Kelly, he spoke from his car to 100,000 persons inside the vast outdoor amphitheater and as many who stood outside on the sidewalks and streets. In that speech he flayed Republican speakers for calling him and his administration "incompetent" and "tired" yet praising their legislation and efforts in building a strong army and navy. (WS)

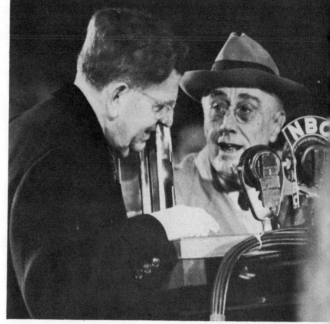

FDR'S OPPONENT Thomas E. Dewey had built a formidable reputation as New York City's crime-busting district attorney and as its state governor, but he was no match for the politically astute President and the prevailing wartime prosperity and increasing battlefront victories. He campaigned diligently, as shown here on his arrival with his wife for a major Chicago speech in which he denounced the administration's strong ties to labor union bosses. (WS)

CHICAGO CELEBRATED as President Truman went on the air on V-E Day, May 8, 1945, to announce that Allied armies had been victorious in Europe. Among the many thousands who cheered were these workers at the Carnegie Illinois Steel Works. (CDN)

[176]   CHARLES de GAULLE, leader of the Free French during World War II and a Chicago visitor shortly after V-E Day, was honored with a parade down State Street as he rode in an open car with Mayor Kelly. Later that day, at a luncheon of civic leaders in the Palmer House, he reminded the United States of its inter-relationship with Europe and warned that unless the wartime affiliation were maintained, Europe might dissolve into chaos. (WS)

A FEW MONTHS later, on August 13, 1945, there was more cause for joy: V-J Day, signalizing Japan's surrender and marked by innumerable festivities, including the gathering of this crowd at State and Madison streets, the "world's busiest corner." (WS)

CALAMITY STRUCK the famous Hotel La Salle when fire raged through the building in the post-midnight hours of June 5, 1946. Property damage came to many millions but, far worse, sixty-one persons lost their lives. A corridor of City Hall, down the block from the hotel, was turned into a makeshift morgue so that friends and relatives of the dead could make identifications wherever possible. (CST-FEA)

THE CRIME OF THE DECADE involved a University of Chicago freshman named William Heirens. He was convicted and sent to Stateville penitentiary in Joliet late in 1946 for the murders of two women and of six-year-old Suzanne Degnan, whose dismembered body was found in North Side sewers. Twenty-six other crimes of his included burglaries, robberies, and assaults. Heirens at first claimed he had nothing to do with the crimes and that a "George Murman" was responsible, but psychiatrists determined that the "other man" was actually part of Heirens' split personality. Ultimately, Heirens became the first inmate of an Illinois penal institution to win a college degree, but was periodically denied parole because of psychiatrists' findings of a "persistent psychological regressiveness." (CST)

FAREWELL TO CAPONE: Late in January 1947, Al Capone was borne to Mount Olivet Cemetery in an inexpensive bronze casket. He had died in his $100,000 Miami Beach villa of a brain hemorrhage eight days after his forty-eighth birthday and several years of paresis. Among the mourners were such former associates as the Fischetti brothers, Charlie and Rocco; Jake Guzik; Sam "Golf Bag" Hunt; and Murray "The Camel" Humphreys. Later his body was transferred to Mount Carmel Cemetery, the grave there topped by a simple headstone inscribed "My Jesus Mercy" until it was stolen in 1972. Upon his death, the *Times* aptly remarked: "What he stood for was a 'public disgrace' because Chicago tolerated him. He became the center of gangland pomp and power, but was a hoodlum to whom this city paid tribute as though he were a leader by choice of the gods. . . . Have we learned our lesson? There is doubt." (WS)

A MAJOR SPORTS EVENT of the 1940s was the winning of the world professional football championship by the Chicago Bears in December 1940. Although the photograph records an event that happened in Washington, it belongs here because it shows George Halas, owner and then-coach, being hoisted on the shoulders of his players after they crushed the Washington Redskins, 73 to 0, to clinch the title. The score was the largest ever recorded in professional football. (CDN)

ANOTHER ATTENTION-GETTER in sports was the 1947 scrap for the middleweight championship between titled Tony Zale (left) and Rocky Graziano on July 16, 1947, in Chicago Stadium. The previous September, Zale had successfully defended his title against Graziano in a blood-gushing battle that ended with a sixth-round knockout. In their second bloody and brutal meeting, Graziano stopped Zale in the sixth round. The two met once more on June 10, 1948, in Newark, New Jersey, where Zale regained the crown with a third-round knockout. Of the Chicago fight, Graziano later said, "This was no boxing match. It was a war, and if there wasn't a referee one of the two of us would have wound up dead." (CST)

AT THE SUGGESTION of the *Tribune,* Chicago staged a Railroad Fair in 1948 to commemorate the 100th anniversary of the first run of William B. Ogden's tiny "Pioneer" locomotive. Maj. Lenox R. Lohr, the guiding genius of the 1933-34 Century of Progress, left his duties as president of the Museum of Science and Industry to direct the fair on a fifty-acre lake-front strip where the Belgian Village and the Streets of Paris had stood fifteen years before. Over two million visited the fair, which offered trains old and new, pageants tracing the development of railroads, and such extra attractions as this Deadwood Central narrow-gauge train on which, for only a dime, passengers could ride the entire length of the fair. The thirty-eight participating railroads derived no profit, but enough goodwill and publicity to make them do a 1949 edition. (MSI)

CHICAGO'S REPUTATION as a maker of entertainment stars continued. Early in 1940, a young comedian named Danny Thomas came from Detroit for a one-week tryout in the 5100 Club on Broadway and remained a solid three years. His distinctive humor ("philosophical comedy, based on the foibles of humanity, eighty per cent dramatic, leading up to an incongruous finish") and such inimitable routines as "Ode to a Wailing Syrian," complete with tablecloth for a burnoose, or his famous story of the hapless fellow with a flat tire and no jack developed a tremendous following. So loyal were his fans that when he made his New York debut—and began a radio-nightclub-theatre-television career of major proportions—a delegation chartered two special train cars to go with him. (DT)

KATHERINE DUNHAM, who earned her doctorate in social anthropology from the University of Chicago in 1937, studied dancing in Brazil and in islands of the Caribbean, and then formed various dance troupes which performed all over the world. Chicago has always been on her itinerary, and here she is as star of her "Tropical Revue" at the Blackstone Theater in 1944. (CST)

FOLLOWING THE TREND set earlier by the "Three Doctors," performers like Dave Garroway maintained a Chicago style in radio that stressed informality, spontaneity, improvisation, and a healthy irreverence. He is shown here in 1945 as he confers with Joe Petrillo, the record-turner on WMAQ's "1160 Club," a regular midnight program on which Garroway offered witty talk between musical numbers. Three years later, when he tried the same technique on his local television show "Garroway at Large," he came to the attention of National Broadcasting Company moguls in New York, and became in 1952 the first host of their "Today" show, a spot he held for a decade before going on to other television and radio ventures. (CST)

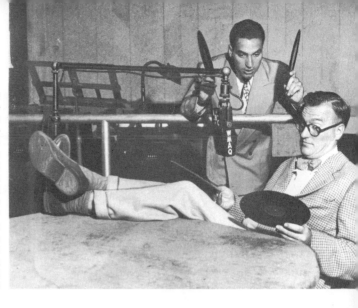

THE HARVEST MOON FESTIVAL, sponsored first by the *Times* and then by the *Sun-Times,* was one of the city's most popular annual events for well over two decades. Musical stars were featured along with winners of dance competitions. This photograph is of a preliminary contest in the very first festival, held in the ballroom of the Skyline Athletic Club in 1945. The newspaper's well-known columnist, Irv "Mr. Chicago" Kupcinet, always served as master of ceremonies. (FEA)

THE SPREAD OF TELEVISION in the late 1940s brought forth new Chicago stars like the Kuklapolitan Players. Favorites then and for years, they were the creation of Burr Tillstrom, seen here with his famous puppets, Kukla and Ollie (the jocular, single-toothed dragon), and the lovely Fran Allison. Originally designed as a program for children, "Kukla, Fran and Ollie" has always had great appeal for adults as well, as is evident whenever it makes periodic reappearances on television. (FEA)

ANOTHER BIG TV FAVORITE was "Studs' Place," a weekly show in which Studs Terkel (front left), later known as "Chicago's Renaissance Man" because of accomplishments in FM radio, the theatre, writing (*Division Street America, Hard Times,* and *Working*), and other arts, played the owner of an informally run restaurant where local characters and visiting celebrities dropped in. Regulars on the show were pianist-raconteur Chet Roble (front right) and, at rear, composer-folksinger Win Stracke and actress Beverly Younger. (KC)

THROUGHOUT THE LAST HALF of the 1940s, many Europeans who had been DPs–displaced persons–managed to come to America and find new homes and new hope. William Sturm of the *Sun-Times* captured the essence of these pilgrimages with this prize-winning photograph of one such group on arrival in the vast Union Station. He titled it "Christmas in the New World." (WS)

THE ELECTIONS OF 1948 included two Chicagoans of high repute as Democratic candidates—Paul H. Douglas (left) and Adlai E. Stevenson, seen here with a "cleanup broom" symbolizing the need to sweep away corruption. Douglas, a former University of Chicago professor who at age fifty-two had given up his seat as alderman to join the Marines, was running for U.S. Senator. Stevenson, a lawyer who had served in the Roosevelt administration, was the party's choice for governor. Neither man was initially given much chance for victory, but that November each won handily, Douglas over C. Wayland "Curly" Brooks, and Stevenson over Dwight "Pete" Green. (KC)

[186]

THIS AERIAL VIEW is of the famous pink-stucco Edgewater Beach Hotel between Sheridan Road and Lake Michigan, shown before the North Lake Shore Drive extension was completed along the lake, thereby dimming the significance of the hotel's name. The hotel itself was demolished early in the 1970s to make way for a high-rise apartment development. (CST)

A NEW GENERATION of realistic Chicago-style writers was emerging. Already established in New York where he had moved in the 1930s after writing the first of his *Studs Lonigan* novels (which drew on his own life and experiences on the city's South Side when it was populated largely by the Irish), was James T. Farrell, shown here on a visit to his home town in 1946. (KC)

NELSON ALGREN wrote his first novel in the 1930s, *Somebody in Boots,* and continued to live and write in Chicago for four decades, turning out fiction which was hailed by Ernest Hemingway and which prompted Carl Sandburg to call him "the poet of the slums." At the end of the 1940s, he completed *The Man With the Golden Arm,* a powerful portrayal of the city's lower depths and of Frankie Machine, a gambler who seeks to break the dope habit. The novel won the first National Book Award for fiction in 1950. (KC)

A STELLAR REPRESENTATIVE of Chicago's naturalistic school of writing was Willard Motley, who had worked with Nelson Algren, Studs Terkel, Jack Conroy, and Saul Bellow on various of the WPA Writers' Projects. He had plugged away for three years before the 1947 publication of his first book *Knock On Any Door,* a rough-tough, yet sympathetic novel about an aggressive young West Sider named Nick Romano whose life-motto is "Live fast, die young and have a good-looking corpse" and who dies in the electric chair for murder. The novel, one of several Motley produced before his death in the early 1960s, was made into a vivid movie starring Humphrey Bogart as the defense attorney. (KC)

[187]

A MAJOR PRIZE-WINNER, also, was Gwendolyn Brooks, a brilliant poet whose first volume *A Street in Bronzeville* appeared in 1945. Five years later she became the first black to be awarded the Pulitzer Prize, for her second collection of poems *Annie Allen.* Shown here after announcement of the award, Miss Brooks has always asserted that her intention as a poet is to "vivify the universal fact . . . but the universal wears contemporary clothing very well." (KC)

EARLY IN THE 1950s, Midway Airport was the world's largest, with fourteen major air lines averaging nine hundred flights daily and carrying nine million passengers annually. (MNP)

INDICATIONS MOUNTED that Midway Airport would be too small for the ever-growing air travel industry. This is a photograph in the 1950s of the tract far to the northwest of the city that became the Chicago-O'Hare International Airport, ten miles square and ten times Midway's size. With the growth of O'Hare as the busiest in the world, Midway became a ghost of its former self, with its facilities used mainly for unscheduled flights, chartered planes, and private craft—and with periodic proposals for its revival. (UA)

THIS DECREPIT BUILDING stood on the site of the Patrick O'Leary dwelling on De Koven Street in whose barn the Great Fire of eighty years before had started. On its front was a plaque installed by the Chicago Historical Society in 1891 that reads: "THE GREAT FIRE OF 1871 ORIGINATED HERE AND EXTENDED TO LINCOLN PARK." Before the 1950s were over, the structure was demolished for new buildings, including the Chicago Fire Department Training Academy. (KC)

A TYPICAL SOUTH SIDE slum alley, doomed to extinction in the urban-renewal programs of the 1950s: One major project was Prairie Shores, which would soon contain five nineteen-story buildings with 1,700 apartments, a private park, shops, and off-street parking facilities. That Prairie Shores adjoined the famous Michael Reese Hospital was instrumental in persuading nearby business and educational institutions, including the Illinois Institute of Technology, to campaign for a vast slum clearance in blighted residential areas. (CDUR)

THE NEAR NORTH SIDE held miserable dwellings areas too. This view is of wornout buildings at the rear of LaSalle Street, their unsafe condition typified by the wooden fire escapes leading to windows. Ultimately, after these and dozens upon dozens of similar structures were eradicated, a vast 1,900-unit apartment and home complex, named for Carl Sandburg, went up in their stead. (CDUR)

THIS VICTORIAN MANSION on Rush Street, in vivid contrast to modern buildings at the rear on North Michigan Avenue, fell to wrecking crews in 1952. Once one of the city's most luxurious houses and known as the "Empress," it was the forty-five-room brownstone residence of the farm-machine multimillionaire Cyrus Hall McCormick. Members of his family occupied it until 1941, after which it stood a flaking, dusty reminder of the grand days when there had been four stately McCormick homes around Rush and Erie streets. Before it was torn down to make way for an apartment building, it was the scene of a macabre "Death of a Mansion" ball staged by students of the Art Institute. (IH)

[191]

SAINT VINCENT DE PAUL CENTER—popularly known as Saint Vincent's Orphanage—ministered
to thousands of unwanted and abandoned youngsters, as typified in this memorable photograph in
the 1950s by Ralph Frost of the *Sun Times*. Founded in a frame house on Orleans Street in 1881, it
occupied an impressive building for half a century on La Salle Street just south of Chicago Avenue,
until it was closed down and its services transferred to other Catholic Charities agencies. (RF)

A FAMILIAR SCENE: Pursued by photographers, Anthony J. "Big Tuna" Accardo, reputed Godfather of the local Mafia syndicate in the 1950s and later, strolls out of police headquarters after a friendly judge orders him released from questioning in connection with an underworld slaying. Besides his status as gangdom's ruler, Accardo, who started his career as a driver-bodyguard for Al Capone, has had the interesting distinction of never having spent a single night in a jail cell. (KC)

RELIEVED OF HIS COMMAND of American forces in Korea by President Truman, in 1951 Gen. Douglas MacArthur made a kind of triumphal tour of major American cities. Here he is at Midway Airport seated beside Mayor Martin J. Kennelly as an enthusiastic admirer breaks watchers' ranks to shake his hand. Kennelly was elected in 1948 as a "reform mayor" after police scandals and other troubles compelled Democratic chieftains to persuade "Big Ed" Kelly not to run again. (CST)

A TRIUMPHANT Dwight D. Eisenhower, Republican 1952 candidate for president, and his wife Mamie (right) stand alongside his vice-presidential running-mate Richard M. Nixon and his wife Pat as they pose happily for photographers in front of the Stevens (later the Conrad Hilton) Hotel after returning from the International Amphitheatre. Not everyone was so instantly happy. Soon, even the *Tribune* was labeling Eisenhower the candidate of Wall Street, and Thomas E. Dewey and the *Tribune's* publisher Col. Robert R. McCormick was allowing as how Eisenhower's chances, no matter whom the Democrats named, were very slim. (CDN)

ADLAI E. STEVENSON, governor of Illinois, was the Democrats' 1952 presidential choice. In this scene recorded by every cameraman amongst the cheering delegates at the International Amphitheatre, incumbent Pres. Harry S. Truman introduced Stevenson. "You have nominated a winner," he cried, "and I am going to take off my coat and do everything I can to help him win!" But Stevenson and his vice-presidential team-mate John Sparkman lost that November, evoking from Stevenson not only congratulations and good wishes for the victors but also a story Abraham Lincoln used to tell: "He said that he felt like a little boy who had stubbed his toe in the dark. He said that he was too old to cry, but it hurt too much to laugh." (RF)

THE DAYS AND NIGHTS were numbered
by the 1950s for Chicago's famous night
club the Chez Paree, whose many attractions included the Chez Paree Adorables,
three of whom appear here in a distinctively
pert number. Opened by Mike Fritzel and
Joey Jacobson in 1932 on Fairbanks Court,
it was a landmark to which the biggest
show-business stars came after appearances
in New York, and was long considered the
only important night club outside Manhattan. High taxes and a trend toward
intimate night spots began causing the
Chez Paree trouble, however, and by 1960
it was shut down. (FT)

A MAJOR BOXING MATCH of 1953—and one of the briefest—was between Rocky Marciano and
Jersey Joe Walcott on May 15 in Chicago Stadium. The previous September in Philadelphia, Walcott,
then world's heavyweight champion, had been knocked out by Marciano in the thirteenth round of a
murderous battle experts claimed was the best heavyweight championship scrap since Jack Dempsey
had licked Luis Angel Firpo twenty-nine years earlier. In the Chicago return match, Marciano knocked
out Walcott the very first round. Here, Walcott is being counted out while holding onto the ropes as
alert cameramen prepare to capture the finish. (RF)

[195]

A CAMPAIGN POSTCARD of November 1954 shows Richard J. Daley, his wife Eleanor—popularly known as Sis—and their seven children when Daley ran for reelection as Cook County Clerk, having served one term after a slow, patient rise through Democratic party ranks. For several years he had been a member of the state legislature and, under Governor Stevenson, state treasurer. The message on the reverse of the card advised recipients to "assist in the election of a fine public official," yet there were already rumors that Daley, having recently assumed the important post of chairman of the Cook County Central Democratic Committee, was aiming toward a more crucial, important position than that of county clerk—mayor of Chicago. (SDS)

MAYOR KENNELLY, aware of Daley's mayoral ambitions, announced in mid-December that he would seek reelection. A week later, however, the party chieftains met and named Daley as the official candidate. The primary was bitter and costly, each man reportedly spending more than $750,000.

When it was over, Daley won by more than 100,000 votes. Kennelly's running mate for city treasurer Morris B. Sachs tearfully consoled Kennelly as the returns were counted, but later agreed to run on the Daley ticket. (CST)

IN THE MAYORAL CONTEST, Daley traversed every neighborhood, even, as shown in this unusual photograph, riding horseback in the Union Stock Yards district. His Republican foe Robert E. Merriam, a onetime Democratic alderman from the University of Chicago ward and an advocate of reform, attacked the Democratic machine as autocratic and corrupt and having strong links with the gambling-crime syndicate. Daley constantly demanded proof of these charges and promised to bring improvements to the city, asserting, "I have talked sense to the people of Chicago. I am confident of their good judgment. (KC)

[197]

ON ELECTION DAY, April 5, 1955, Daley defeated Merriam by 127,000 votes, and in due time was sworn into office by his old friend Judge Abraham Lincoln Marovitz, while Martin Kennelly, the outgoing Democratic mayor who had taken no part in the fight, stood sadly by. Daley's inaugural statement was predictable: "I will make this city a better and more beautiful place to live." But imbedded more deeply into Chicago's lore was what the city's perkiest alderman, Mathias "Paddy" Bauler, had to say: "Chicago ain't ready for reform!" (CDN)

THE DALEY ERA BEGINS: On his first day as Chicago's new mayor, Richard J. Daley pauses in City Hall to pose in front of an aerial view of his domain. In ensuing years, he would serve longer as mayor than anyone else in the city's history, arousing great praise and loyalty and great criticism and bitterness, developing immense power locally and nationally, creating new legends and firm realities and, in myriad ways, reshaping and remolding the city. (KC)

Index

Accardo, Anthony J. "Big Tuna," 193
Addams, Jane, 59, 96, 97, 149
Ade, George, 58
Adler, Dankmar, 52, 53, 69
Algren, Nelson, 187
Allen, Jane Addams, 10
Allison, Fran, 184
Altgeld, Gov. John Peter, 47
American, 18, 131
Anderson, Gilbert M. "Bronco Billy," 105
Anderson, Herbert L., 170
Andreas, A. T., 15
Anselmi, Albert, 127
Anson, Adrian "Cap," 56
Arbeiter Zeitung, 47
Armour, Philip, 65
Art Institute, 66, 111, 117, 191
Arts Club, 119
Astor, John Jacob, 17
Auditorium, 52
Avery, Sewell, 174

Balbo, Gen. Italo, 154
Balestier, Joseph N., 18
Barry, Dave, 130
Bauler, Mathias "Paddy," 197
Bayne, Beverly, 105
Beale, Joseph Boggs, 56
Beaubien, Jean, 17
Beaubien, Mark, 17, 27
Beery, Wallace, 105
Behmiller, Helen, 163
Bell Building, 140
Bellow, Saul, 187
Beman, Solon H., 69
Bernhardt, Sarah, 35
Black Hawk, 16
Board of Trade building, 38, 49

Bodenheim, Maxwell, 131
Borden, Mary, 116
Boucree, Gladys, 164
Boyington, William W., 48
Bradbury, Ray, 163
Braddock, James J., 156
Brooks, Sen. C. Wayland "Curly," 186
Brooks, Gwendolyn, 187
Bross, William "Deacon," 34
Buck, Thomas, 10
Buckingham Fountain, 135
Burley, Rev. William, 85
Burnham, Daniel H., 51, 69, 94, 95, 122, 126
Burns, Thomas, 10
Bushman, the gorilla, 145
Bushman, Francis X., 105

Cabrini, Frances, 149
Caldwell, Billy (Sauganash), 17
Camp Douglas, 29
Canzoneri, Tony, 156
Capone, Al, 115, 126, 127, 143, 158, 179, 193
Carleton, Will, 29
Carnegie Illinois Steel Works, 176
Carter, Caroline Louise Dudley (Mrs. Leslie), 77
Carter, Leslie, 77
Cass, Lewis, 14
Castle, Irene, 166
Cavalier, Robert, sieur de la Salle, 12
Century of Progress exposition, 148-49, 151-4, 181
Cermak, Anton J. "Tony," 146, 147
Chamber of Commerce Building, 38
Cheecheebingway, 16
Chez Paree, 195
Chicagoan, 123
Chicago Allied Arts, 137
Chicago and Atlantic Railway, 55

Chicago and Northwestern Railway, 21, 48
Chicago City Railway Company, 44
Chicago Cubs, 56, 90, 157
Chicago Dock Company, 77
Chicago Elevated Railroad, 77
Chicago Fire Department Training Academy, 19(
Chicago Freight Tunnel, 144
Chicago Historical Society, 190
Chicago Journal, 74
Chicago Literary Times, 131
Chicago Motor Coach Company, 125
Chicago Plan Commission, 94, 115, 122
Chicago Press Photographers Association, 9
Chicago Public Library, 37, 51, 117
Chicago Rapid Transit Company, 173
Chicago Stadium, 146, 167, 175, 180, 195
Chicago Stock Exchange, 53
Chicago Sun, 172
Chicago Symphony Orchestra, 66, 173
Chicago Telephone Company, 45, 83, 105
Chicago Times-Herald, 79
City Hall, 20, 33, 37, 50, 51, 178
Civic Opera House, 137
Coliseum, 58, 73, 157
Clark, Bennett Champ, 174
Cleveland, Pres. Grover, 76
Cobb, Henry Ives, 54, 69, 81
Cody, "Buffalo Bill," 43
Coleman, Harry, 154
Collins, Charles, 131
Colosimo, "Big Jim," 126
Comiskey, Charles, 90
Comiskey Park, 133, 156
Compton, Arthur Holly, 170
Conroy, Jack, 187
Cook County Jail, 128, 159
Cooper, Maurice, 164
Correll, Charles, 136
Coughlin, John "Bathhouse John," 73, 98, 100
Courthouse, 19, 30, 33
Crane, R. T., 39
Cross, Milton J., 136
Crowe, Robert E., 128
Cubs Park, 90
Cunningham, Patrick, 10
Cuyler, Hazen "Kiki," 130

Daily News, 9, 71, 122, 125, 128, 131, 135
Daley, Richard Joseph, 151, 196, 197, 198
Daley, Eleanor & family, 196
Dana, Charles, 68
Daneluk, J. P., 10
Darrow, Clarence, 72, 128
Davis, Jefferson, 16
Davis, Judge David F., 28
Davis, Phillip R., 131
Davis, Theodore R., 31
Dawes, Charles G., 94
Dawes, Mrs. Rufus C., 154
Dawes, Rufus C., 148, 149, 154
Dean, Jerome "Dizzy," 157

Dearborn, Henry, 14
Dearborn Street Depot, 102, 165
Debs, Eugene V., 76, 77
Dedmon, Emmett, 9
de Gaulle, Charles, 176
DeLamarter, Eric, 137
Democrat, 18, 23
Dempsey, Jack, 126, 130, 195
DeSanti, Shirlee, 9
D'Esposito, Joshua, 173
Dever, Mayor William E., 123, 132
Dewey, Thomas E., 175, 194
Dillinger, John, 158
Disraeli, Benjamin, 37
Douglas, Paul H., 186
Douglas, Stephen A., 18, 21, 29
Draeger, Harlan, 9
Drake Hotel, 118
Dreiser, Theodore, 70
Dunham, Katherine, 182
Dunne, Edward F., 82
Dunne, Finley Peter, 58
Duryea, Charles, 78
Duryea, Frank, 78, 85
duSable, Jean Baptiste Pointe, 13

Eagle Exchange, 17
Eastland, 104
Eckhardt, Fred, 104
Edgewater Beach Hotel, 186
Eisenhower, Pres. Dwight D., 194
Eisenhower, Mamie, 194
Eliot, T. S., 131
Ellsworth, Col. Elmer E., 28
Engel, George, 47
Essanay Company, 105
Evans, Silliman, 172
Evening American, 137
Everleigh, Ada & Minna, 98, 99, 100

Fallon, B. J., 173
Falstein, Maurie, 9
Farrell, James T., 187
Farwell, John V., 94
Federal Building, 81
Fermi, Enrico, 170
Ferris, George, 71
Field, Eugene, 58, 71
Field, Marshall, 26, 27, 65, 126
Field, Marshall, III, 172
Field Museum of Natural History, 70, 145, 152
Fielden, Samuel "Good-natured Sam," 47
Fifer, Gov. Joseph, 52
Finnegan, Richard J., 167
Firpo, Luis Angel, 195
Fischer, Adolph, 47
Fischetti, Charles & Rocco, 179
Fishbein, Dr. Morris, 131
Flynn, Bernadine, 163
Fort Dearborn, 14, 15, 16, 17, 24, 116
Foy, Eddie, 80

Fox, Charles, 118
Fraction, Edward, 164
Frances Cabrini Homes, 149
Frank, Dutch, 25
Frank Parmelee Transfer System, 102
Franks, Bobby, 128
Friedrich, Charlie, 65
Fritzel, Mike, 195
Frost, Ralph, 9, 151, 192
Frost, Robert, 131

Galena & Chicago Railroad, 20
Garbo, Greta, 144
Garden, Mary, 136
Gardiner, Charles "Chuck," 157
Garrick Building, 53
Garroway, Dave, 183
Garry, Thomas Dennis, 167
Gaston, Lucy Page, 99
Gebardi, Vincent, 158
Genna, Angelo, Tony, and Mike, 127
George III, 13
Goldstein, Alvin, 128
Goodman, Benny, 164
Gorman, Alice, 10
Gosden, Freeman, 136
Grange, Harold "Red," 129
Grant Park, 66, 70, 78, 116, 126, 135, 152
Graziano, Rocky, 180
Great Fire of 1871, 29, 31-40, 155
Grebe shipyards, 171
Green, Gov. Dwight "Pete," 186
Grimm, Charlie, 147
Gunther, Charles F., 58
Gunther, John, 131
Gusenberg; Frank & Pete, 127
Guske, Ellen, 10
Gusik, Jake, 179

Halas, George, 180
Hamm, Russell V., 128
Hankins, John, 19
Harlan, John M., 82
Harlow, Jean, 144
Harper, William Rainey, 80, 108
Harrington, Philip J., 173
Harrison, Carter Henry the Younger, 82, 100
Harrison, Mayor Carter Henry, 42, 43, 72, 82
Harrison, Pres. Benjamin, 52
Hartnett, Leo "Gabby," 157
Hartzell, Clarence L., 163
Haymarket Square, 36, 47
Heald, Capt. Nathan, 14, 16
Heald, Rebekah (Mrs. Nathan), 16
Hecht, Ben, 131
Heinlein, Robert D., 10
Heirens, William, 179
Helms, Mrs. Margaret, 14
Hennigs, Mrs. Armin, 9
Herald-Examiner, 137, 144, 151
Herguth, Bob, 9

Hesler, Alexander, 24
Hilberry, Norman, 170
Hill, John, 25
Hill, Mary, 25
Hines, Thomas, 29
Hitler, Adolf, 161, 162
Holmes, Henry H., 74
Home Insurance Company, 51
Honore, Bertha, 54
Hood, Raymond M., 119
Hoover, Pres. Herbert, 146
Hopkins, Mayor John "Dapper Johnny," 74
Horner, Gov. Henry, 147
Hornsby, Rogers, 130
Horton, D. F., 34
Hoyt, William H., building, 64
Hubbard, Gurdon S., 18
Hull, Charles J., 59
Hull, Gen. William, 14
Hull House, 59, 96, 97
Humphreys, Murray "The Camel," 179
Hunt, Richard Morton, 69
Hunt, Sam "Golf Bag," 179
Hutchins, Robert Maynard, 139
Hutchinson, Charles, 50
Hyer, Adam, 127

Ida B. Wells Homes, 149
Idelson, Bill, 163
Illinois Athletic Club, 117
Illinois Central Railroad, 21, 30, 34, 78
Illinois Institute of Technology, 190
International Amphitheatre, 194
Insull, Samuel, 137, 159
Interstate Industrial Exposition building, 39
Iroquois Theater, 80

Jackson Park, 67, 68, 71, 92, 93, 114
Jackson, William Henry, 101, 102
Jacobson, Joey, 195
Jane Addams Homes, 149
Jeffers, Robinson, 131
Jefferson, Joseph, 43
Jenney, William LeBaron, 51, 52
Joliet, Louis, 11, 12, 16
Jordan, Jim & Marian, 163
Joyce, James, 131

Kanter, Borrie, 167
Kaufmann & Fabry, 10
Kavanagh, Marcus, 78
Kelly, Edward J. "Big Ed," 147, 167, 173, 175,
    176, 193
Kenna, Michael "Hinky Dink," 73, 97,98, 100
Kennelly, Mayor Martin J., 193, 196, 197
Kenney, Edward, 50
Kerfoot, William D., 36
Kimball Building, 66
King of the Sandwich Islands, 39
King, Wayne, 164
Kinzie family, 16'

Kinzie, John, 13, 14, 15, 18
Kinzie, John, Jr., 18
Kogan, Marilew, 10
Kogan, Mark, 10
Kohlsaat, Hermann H., 78
Kopriva, Ben, 9
Kotalik, George, 170
Kotalik, Robert, 9
Kuhn, Fritz, 162
Kupcinet, Irv "Mr. Chicago," 183
KYW, radio station, 136

Lake Shore & Michigan Southern, 38
Lardner, Ring, 105
La Salle, Hotel, 178
La Salle Street Station, 167
Laubenheimer, Henry C. W., 143
Lawrence, D. H., 131
Lawrence, George R. "Flashlight," 91
Leavitt, Wellington, 132
Leiter, Levi Z., 26, 27
Le Lime, Jean, 13, 14
Leopold, Nathan, 128
Levee, 98, 99, 100
Lewis, Janice, 9
Lewis, John L., 160
Lewis, Lloyd, 131
Libby Prison, 58
Liebling, A. J., 151
Lincoln, Abraham, 27, 28, 30, 194
Lincoln Park, 34, 92, 125, 145
Lindbergh, Charles Augustus, 133, 134
Lingg, Louis, 47
Literary Digest, 149
Loeb, Richard, 128
Lohr, Lenox, 149, 181
London Guarantee Building, 140
Loop, 63
Louis XIV, 12
Louis, Joe, 156
Lowden, Frank O., 126
Lowell, Amy, 131
Lundin, Fred "Poor Swede," 128

MacArthur, Gen. Douglas, 193
McCambridge, Mercedes, 163
McCarthy, Joe, 130, 147
McCormick, Col. Robert Rutherford, 172, 194
McCormick, Cyrus Hall, 22, 39, 191
McCormick, Edith Rockfeller, 138
McCormick, Harold, 138
McCormick Harvester Works, 46
McCree, Marilyn, 10
McCutcheon, John T., 58
McDonald, Eugene, 144
McDonald, Michael Cassius "King Mike," 42
McGill, Edward, 9, 145, 166
McGuire, Peter J., 89
McGurn, Jack "Machine Gun," 158
Mack, Connie, 130
McLaughlin, Frederic, 166
MacLeish, Archibald, 131

McSwiggin, William J., 127
Mahzar, Fareeda, 71
Mann, David, 145
March, Mush, 157
Marciano, Rocky, 195
Markey, Morris, 117
Marovitz, Judge Abraham Lincoln, 197
Marquette, Fr. Jacques, 11, 12, 116
Marshall, Benjamin, 118
Marshall Field and Company, 101
Martineau, Harriet, 18-19
Marx, Gustav, 81
Masonic Temple, 61
Mason, Mayor Roswell B., 34
Masters, Edgar Lee, 115, 131
Maxwell Street Market, 142
May, John, 127
Medill, Joseph, 28
Medinah Athletic Club, 140
Merriam, Robert E., 197
Michael Reese Hospital, 190
Midway Airport, 134, 151, 188, 189, 193
Midway Gardens, 106
Mill, John Stuart, 37
Millay, Edna St. Vincent, 131
Monroe Building, 117
Monroe, Harriet, 131
Montgomery Ward and Company, 41, 66, 168, 169, 174
Moody, Mrs. William Vaughn, 166
Moran, George "Bugs," 127
Morris, Buckner S., 29
Motley, Willard, 187
Mount Carmel Cemetery, 178
Mudgett, Herman, 74
Mulroy, James, 128
Mundelein, George, Cardinal, 161
Municipal Airport, 133, 134
Municipal (later Navy) Pier, 108
Museum of Science and Industry, 70, 126, 139, 181

Nash, Patrick J., 147
Navy Pier, 108
Neebe, Oscar W., 47
Newberry & Dole, 22
Newspaper Alley, 58
Niedemeyer, Peter, 81
Nixon, Pat, 194
Nixon, Richard M., 194
Norris, Frank, 49
North Michigan Avenue Building (333), 140

Oakley, Annie, 72
Oakwoods Cemetery, 29
O'Banion, Dion, 127
O'Brien, Joseph, 10
O'Connor, Thomas "Terrible Tommy," 128
O'Donnell, Klondike, 127
Ogden, Mayor William B., 19, 20, 21, 23, 181
O'Leary, Patrick and Catherine, 29, 32, 190
O'Neill, Sgt. Patrick J., 128
Ouilmette, Antoine, 10

Page, Ruth, 137
Palace Car Company, 55
Palmer, Gov. John, 34
Palmer House, 26, 40, 124, 176
Palmer, Potter, 26, 27, 39, 54, 81
Parish, George, Jr., 15
Parker, Alfred E., 145
Parks, Berenice, 164
Parkway Community House, 171
Parmelee, Frank, 102
Parrish, Douglas M., 170
Parsons, Albert R., 47
Patti, Adelina, 52
Pauer, William, 174
Peck, Ferdinand Whyte, 52
Peebles, George, 9, 135
Peesotum, 14
Peoples Gas Light and Coke Company, 125
Peterson, Arthur, 163
Petrillo, Joe, 183
Phillips, Wally, 10
Pinet, Fr. Francois, 12
Poetry, 131
Pound, Ezra, 131
Post, Wiley, 134
Powers, John "Johnny De Pow," 97
Pratt, Russell, 162
Prendergast, Patrick Eugene, 72
Preston, Keith, 131
Prince of Wales, 132
Pullman, George M., 27, 55, 65, 75, 76
Pure Oil Building, 140

Quaife, Milo M., 13
Queen Victoria, 37
Quinn, James, 173
Quinn, Jimmy, 144

Raisa, Rosa, 137
Rand, Sally, 150, 151
Read, Opie, 58
Republic Steel Corporation, 160
Rhymer, Paul, 163
Rice, Wallace, 58
Riverview, 107
Robinson, Alexander (Cheecheebingway), 16
Robinson, Ernest, 85
Robinson, Marjorie, 185
Roble, Chet, 184
Rochford, James M., 10
Rockefeller, John D., 80, 138
Rock Island & Pacific, 38
Roebuck, Alvah C., 87
Roeski, Emil, 81
Rookery, 51
Roosevelt, Pres. Franklin Delano, 146, 147, 161,
    167, 174, 175
Roosevelt, Pres. Theodore, 80
Root, George F., 27, 34
Root, John W., 51, 69
Rosenwald, Julius, 87, 139
Ross, Barney, 156

Rossetti, Dante Gabriel, 37
Rudolph, Joe, 162
Ruskin, John, 119
Ruth, Babe, 147

Saarinen, Eliel, 119
Sachs, Morris B., 196
Sage, Anna, 158
St. Gaudens, Augustus, 70
Saint Vincent's Orphanage, 192
Sandburg, Carl, 131, 187, 191
Sands, 19, 25
Sans Souci, 106
Scalisi, John, 127
Schnabel, Artur, 173
Schoolcraft, Henry, 14
Schreiber, Mignon, 163
Schwab, Michael, 47
Schwimmer, Dr. Reinhart, 127
Scott, Gen. Winfield, 16
Sears, Richard W., 87
Selig Film Company, 105
Seward, William H., 28
Sheil, Bishop Bernard J., 161
Shedd, John G., 94
Sheridan, Gen. Philip H., 34
Sherman Hotel, 24, 109
Sherman, Ransom, 162
Shortall, John G., 33
Sinclair, Upton, 89
Smith, Gipsy, 99
Smith, Al, 156
Smith, Henry Justin, 131
Snyder, John W., 174
Sparkman, John, 194
Spies, August, 47
Spoor, George K., 105
Stagg, Amos Alonzo, 108
Starr, Ellen Gates, 59
Stead, William T., 67, 99
Stein, Eugene I., Jr., 10
Stephenson, Riggs, 130
Stevens, Ashton, 131
Stevenson, Adlai E., 186, 194
Stock, Frederick, 173
Stracke, Win, 184
Streeter, George Wellington "Cap," 103
Sturm, William, 9, 185
Sullivan, Louis Henri, 52, 53, 69, 106, 117
Sun-Times, 9, 172, 183, 185, 192
Sutter, J. B., 10
Swanson, Gloria, 105
Swearingen, Lt. James Strode, 15
Sweet, Col. Benjamin J., 29
Sweitzer, Robert, 103, 114
Swift, Gustavus F., 132
Swift, Louis F., 132
Swoiskin, Lenore, 10
Szilard, Leo, 170

Tagore, Rabindranath, 131

Teasdale, Sara, 131
Terkel, Studs, 184, 187
Theatre Alley, 43
Thom, Robert, 12
Thomas, Danny, 182
Thomas, Theodore, 66
Thompson, Bill, 163
Thompson, James, 18
Thompson, Mayor William "Big Bill," 68, 110,
    114, 115, 116, 128, 132, 134, 146
Thorne, George R., 41
Tillstrom, Burr, 184
Times, 57, 167, 170, 172, 174, 179, 183
Torrio, Johnny, 126, 127
Tower Building, 117
Tribune, 25, 26, 27, 28, 37, 128, 136, 145, 172,
    181, 194
Tribune Tower, 119, 140, 172
Truman, Pres. Harry S., 174, 176, 193
Tunney, Gene, 126, 130
Turpin, Ben, 105

United Air Lines, 134
University Club, 117
University of Chicago, 80, 108, 139, 151, 170
Union Station, 123, 144, 185
Union Stock Yards, 22, 30, 35, 88, 89, 91, 132,
    155, 197

Van Dine, Harvey, 81
Van Grove, Isaac, 136
Van Harvey, Art, 163
Van Osdel, John, 50
Vicini, Tina, 10

Wacker, Charles H., 94, 122
Walcott, "Jersey Joe," 195
Walker, James T., 132
Walsh, Charles, 29
Walsh, Frank J., 158
Walska, Ganna, 138
Ward, A. Montgomery, 41, 66, 117
Ward, Police Capt. William, 47
Washington Park, 57, 71
Washington Park Racetrack, 57
Water Tower, 118, 125
Wayne, Gen. Anthony "Mad Anthony," 13
Wees, Patricia M., 10
Wehner, Don, 9
Weil, George, 170
Weinshank, Alfred, 127
Weiss, Hymie, 127
Weissmuller, Johnny, 129
Wells, Ida B., 149
Wells, Capt. William, 14
Wendt, Lloyd, 9
WENR, radio station, 163
Wentworth, Mayor John "Long John," 25, 26
West, Mae, 144
Western Electric Company, 104
Wetten, Emil C., 147

WGN, radio station, 156
Whistler, Capt. John, 13, 14, 15
White City, 107
Whitechapel Club, 58
White Sox, 90, 133
White Stockings Park, 56
Whitlock, Brand, 58
Wigner, E. P., 170
Wigwam, 28
Willkie, Wendell, 167
Willoughby Building, 117
Wilson, Edmund, 141
Wilson, Lewis "Hack," 130
Wilson, Woodrow, 110
Winch, Art, 156
WMAQ, radio station, 136, 183
World's Columbian Exposition, 36, 66, 67, 68,
    69, 70, 71, 72, 73, 75, 107, 139, 149, 152
Wright, Frank Lloyd, 106
Wright, John Stephen, 17, 22, 34
Wrigley Building, 119, 140
Wrigley Field, 147
Wrigley, William, 119, 132
Wynekoop, Dr. Alice Lindsay, 159

Yeats, William Butler, 131
Yerkes, Charles Tyson, 44
Younger, Beverly, 184

Zale, Tony, 180
Zinn, Walter H., 170